WHAT PEOPLE ARE SAYING ABOUT THIS BOOK!

This book is written to work as a key to unlock your next steps propelling you into your new season of destiny.

Whenever God is wanting to move us forward He will place tools in our hands to bring the revelation we need to see clearly and then to step. This book is one of those very tools! I have had the pleasure of knowing Rev. Shonna Slatten for the last 5 years, during that time she has taken part with us in international events that our ministry has hosted. I have found her to be an excellent living example of a heart after God and a heart after destiny. She is well equipped to speak to what it takes to live a life of destiny with insight and clarity. You will no doubt be elevated from reading this book, "It's In You" receiving a new grace for your race and equipped for all that lies ahead on your path of destiny.

JEN TRINGALE

JEN TRINGALE MINISTRIES

Shonna has been a tremendous blessing in our lives, and not only is she one of the most faithful people we know to the Word of God, she carries a mighty gift as an exhorter and encourager. This book speaks to destiny, identity, creativity, enlarging, ability and knowing through the power of God that is in each of us. Through the lives of servants and saints from Scriptures, and from Shonna's own personal experiences, she unfolds the attributes God has placed in each of us to fulfill His purposes for our lives. God is always equipping and qualifying us for an eternal position, and Shonna's book leads us into His destiny for our lives. It's in YOU!

Pastors Bob and Brenda Greene
The Calling Church Norman, Oklahoma

Shonna is the real deal! She devours God's Word and delivers it with a contagious passion. Shonna ingests fresh revelation then ignites a fire in others to pursue where God is leading. These pages possess that same fire. Too many folks become comfortable in their discomfort. Consequently, they miss what awaits on the other side of struggle. "Destiny Etched Within" extends multiplied help and hope for those who want to experience all God dreamed for them but can't seem to get there. It's time! It's for YOU! Grab hold of this life-altering book and don't let go until you catch her passion and burn with the fire in its unfolding!

Pastor Debbie Lanier
Hope Community Church
Winston-Salem, North Carolina

The first paragraph of the Introduction nailed me! I know that's probably not how to begin a recommendation for a book, but I really mean it. When you move in the Prophetic, you are continuously in transition. We move from "glory to glory," but seldom are those "Glories" connected. There is usually an awkward place of faith in between. In her new book, "Destiny Etched Within,"

Shonna Slatten confronts those awkward places of faith, and not only does she speak into them, but she speaks out from them, as well!

Our family has traveled with Shonna internationally and witnessed her passion for His Presence. Whether it's Latin America or Northern Nigeria, Africa, Shonna possesses a Divine Dissatisfaction and is determined to press into the Next of God. You're going to want to go along with her!

PAUL FRANCIS LANIER
HOPE COMMUNITY CHURCH
WINSTON-SALEM, NORTH CAROLINA

One of the most beneficial, liberating, and empowering revelations that a believer can possess, particularly in the communication of their faith - is the "acknowledging of every good thing that is in them in Christ." (Philemon 1:6) However, it is not merely the acknowledging of these attributes, but embracing them and walking in their reality that propels one forward in the apprehension of their divine destiny. Within the pages of this book, Shonna gives practical insight and spiritual principles that will enable you to not only identify, but develop, release and sustain your God given gifts and potential. Each chapter enables you to unwrap another facet of this wonderful God-created package called "you"! Enjoy the discovery!

MARTY BLACKWELDER
PRESIDENT OF BLACKWELDER MINISTRIES

FOREWORD BY DONNA SCHAMBACH

DESTINY ETCHED WITHIN

How to Get Empowered with Purpose

SHONNA SLATTEN

emerge
publishing

TULSA, OKLAHOMA

23 22 21 20 19 18   8 7 6 5 4 3 2 1

DESTINY ETCHED WITHIN— How to Get Empowered with Purpose
Copyright © 2018 Shonna Slatten

Scripture quotations marked (AMP) are taken from the Amplified Bible, Copyright © 1954, 1958, 1962, 1964, 1965, 1987 by The Lockman Foundation. Used by permission.

Scripture quotations taken from the New American Standard Bible® (NASB), Copyright © 1960, 1962, 1963, 1968, 1971, 1972, 1973, 1975, 1977, 1995 by The Lockman Foundation Used by permission. www.Lockman.org

emerge
publishing
TULSA, OKLAHOMA

Published by:
Emerge Publishing, LLC
9521B Riverside Parkway, Suite 243
Tulsa, Oklahoma 74137
Phone: 888.407.4447
www.EmergePublishing.com

Library of Congress Cataloging-in-Publication Data

ISBN: 978-1-943127-75-7 Paperback
ISBN: 978-1-943127-76-4 Digital/E-book

BISAC Category:
REL012070   RELIGION / Christian Life / Personal Growth
REL012130   RELIGION / Christian Life / Women's Issues
REL012120   RELIGION / Christian Life / Spiritual Growth

Printed in the United States

CONTENTS

THIS BOOK IS DEDICATED TO:

My father, Lee Slatten and my stepmother Patty Slatten. My dad has been my biggest encourager, pillar and strength in my life. Dad, you are a man of wisdom who has led by example and taught me well. I love you.

My mother, Toni Eads, and my stepfather, Gene Eads, both of whom encourage me greatly. Gene, you have been a strong example of keeping the faith through trying circumstances; always persevering and believing the best. I love you both.

My Grandmother, Dolores Slatten, who was a great inspiration to me. She poured her life into me and helped me discover many of my gifts and talents, and always cheered me on to run with them. I love you beyond expression.

My pastors, Bob and Brenda Greene, who have also been a great inspiration in my life. Brenda specifically has been my mentor and spiritual mom. Thank you for pouring your life into me and always being here for me, encouraging me, challenging me, and bringing out the excellence in me. I love you big.

All my family and friends for being a great support to me in all my endeavors. All of you are very special and dear to me. I love and cherish you.

FOREWORD

For over a decade now, I have known Shonna Slatten as a vibrant life force for the Kingdom of God. She is bold; she is passionate; and she is gifted with the ability to encourage faith in the lives of everyone she touches.

I have had many conversations with my dear friend Shonna. Her life has been forged on the oil press. She has faced real giants and life-altering discouragements, and yet she has come out shining and shouting. Shonna is a woman of faith who has a calling and passion to see others rise above their own life issues, and be everything God has destined them to be.

Destiny Etched Within is a book written from the heart of a tried vessel of honor. With wisdom and sound biblical instruction, Shonna helps the reader understand how to not only recognize and understand spiritual destiny, but also how to release that destiny, by the power of the Holy Spirit.

You will be challenged—you will be lifted—and I believe with all my heart, you will soar as you allow the Spirit to have His perfect way in you, while pouring over the pages of this inspiring book.

DONNA SCHAMBACH
PRESIDENT/CEO OF SCHAMBACH MINISTRIES
AUTHOR, THE ANOINTING FOR MIRACLES

INTRODUCTION

Have you ever found yourself in a place in your life that you were discontent with the season you were in? You had to ask, Is this all there is for me Lord? You know there is more, but you don't quite know how to step into it. If you look at the world around you with your natural eyes, it can seem fearsome and threatening. But when you look through the eyes of your spirit, a new fire of excitement goes off, and it begins to build on the inside of you.

God has seasons for each one of us, and moving into a new season is not always easy. But, if you've noticed, God is all about change and advancing us to the next level and season. He is all about new experiences to give us opportunities to grow.

A new season means God wants to do a greater work in you and through you. There are new things He wants you to take possession of and establish. As He states in Isaiah:

"Stop dwelling on past events and brooding over times gone by; I am doing something new; it's springing up – can't you see it? I am making a road in the desert, rivers in the wasteland." Isa. 43:18-19 (CJB)

"Forget the former things; do not dwell on the past. For I am about to do something new. See, I have already begun! Do you not see it? I will make a pathway through the wilderness. I will create rivers in the dry wasteland."

Isa. 43:18-19 (NLT)

The word new is an interesting word. A new thing can be happening, but in the midst of a beginning, we can fail to perceive the change. Remember, an end always precedes a beginning. Therefore, the question becomes: How are you reacting when an end comes, and a new beginning starts? How will you react to this new thing God is doing? Will you respond to this new season in your life? Or will you dismiss it because of fear? For certain, it involves change. Some people are more apt to welcome change; others loathe it. But, even for those who like change, it's often easy to stay in the same place just because it's familiar and comfortable. You know how to function in that familiar place. It's easier to stay in the same place, simply because you don't have to put forth greater effort and it's predictable.

But, something inside you is compelling you, and you can no longer stay in the place that never changes; because you know deep inside you that there's more that God wants to do. You know you must move into the more.

God is a progressive God. He is continually leading you into new challenges and new adventures. His plan is for each of us to continually grow and move forward in His purposes for our lives and to build and establish His Kingdom. To have God's highest and best in our lives, we have to move forward in some things, and we have to let go of other things that are no longer necessary.

Often, there is a period of transition. In other words, we know God is telling us to let go of—whatever it is. But, He's not yet revealed that to which we are moving into. That is an unsettling place because it's the unknown. It's a place I call the hallway—the place where you have let go of the old, but the new door has not opened yet. It is a place of trust and process in your life.

In this book, I want to share my journey and explore the lives of some of the most faithful, loyal and gifted people in the Bible. I share some things that I have learned in my walk thus far, but by no means have arrived. I have learned the more I know, the less I know, and how dependent I am on the Great Teacher to teach and lead me through this journey of life. I reveal that these faithful Bible people didn't know they had everything they needed inside of them for their new season—not until God revealed their true identities and abilities to them.

There is a destiny in every person that must be discovered. All of us have gifts, abilities, and strengths within us waiting to be discovered. God wants to remove the fear and the excuses that hold us back. He wants to unveil the beauty and authenticity of our true selves. He wants to unlock the masterpiece within us so that He can move us into a new thing.

You will also find out in this book that no matter where God is leading, no matter what new thing He has for you, no matter how He's propelling you into your destiny, you are well able to walk this path. You are well able to possess the land He places before you as you activate principles and give voice to decreeing His Word.

God has deposited inside you everything you need. You need to be fully persuaded of that and believe He is able to perform that which He has said about your destiny. My prayer is that you will have a greater revelation of the deposits and the destiny etched within—that confidence rises in you from God revealing your true identity and the power you carry.

My hope is that this book will help you discover many strengths that are lying dormant inside of you. That you will see your challenges as opportunities for growth, faith-enrichment, and promotion. I hope you will be inspired and encouraged to apply these principles and enlarge yourself to move into the new season and enjoy the destiny God has etched within you. May the Spirit of God illuminate your life through these pages revealing your potential and the rich deposits on the inside of you so that you can declare, "It's in me!"

It's in YOU!

CHAPTER ONE

INTIMACY

On November 5th, at eleven o'clock at night, 1996, I experienced an encounter with God, which forever changed the trajectory of my life and launched me on a journey of intimacy with the Father on a level I had never known before. It was that night that I came to the end of myself and everything I was about and fully surrendered all to the Lord Jesus. I told him to take my life and make me the woman He has called me to be.

With joyful tears that night, I truly felt myself die and come into a new place with my Savior. I became a new creature in Christ Jesus; all things passed away, and all things had become new. Jesus had been my Savior since I was six years old, but that night He became my Lord. As I surrendered all to Him, He became Lord over everything in my life from that point on. That was the birthing place of my journey with Jesus—my Lord, my Master, my Savior, my Life.

It was in this place I was introduced to the Holy One living inside me—the Holy Spirit, my Comforter, my Helper, my Counselor, my Advocate and my Encourager. It was in this encounter, this experience with Holy Spirit that changed the course of my life and my destiny.

The Spirit of God began wooing me into the secret place of the Most High to dwell with Him. I would awaken every morning, and He was there waiting to fellowship and minister to me. He became so real to me. Every day, as I would open the Bible and read the Word of God, tears would flow as I experienced the Living Word coming alive, flying off the pages to me, answering questions I didn't even know I had.

We met every day for hours and hours. It seemed I was in His presence for only a few minutes, but before I knew it, half the day had gone by. It seemed I had awakened an appetite I had never experienced in my life. A hunger was surging through me to know Him along with a thirst for His Living Water. Every morning I heard Him say, "Beloved, my daughter, come away with me." And, I did. I would lay out the pieces of my life on the altar and wait for His fire to fall upon my heart. Our intimacy and relationship were birthed as He told me, "Into me, you will see, for that is true intimacy, and I will reveal to you, your true identity."

During a natural birth, there may be others in attendance; however, rarely are others around during the conception. It's private; it's intimate, it's in the "secret place." So, you may ask, why are not more dreams, visions, and ideas not coming to light? It may be because the first key step has been overlooked, ignored, omitted, or cast aside. That is dwelling in the secret place of the Most High. That is where conception takes place and dreams are birthed.

MAKE LIFE ABOUT KNOWING HIM

Intimacy is all about knowing God and practicing His presence. It's about knowing His ways and becoming skillful in the Word and the ways of the Spirit.

Our relationship to the Word of God is directly related to our relationship with the Lord. He is the Word made flesh. Spending time in the Lord's presence, and being in His Word, go hand and hand. His Word reveals who He is. We should place great value on the Word and abide in it, for that is where we will hear His voice. As we abide by the Word, much fruit will abound to our account.

The reason God calls us to sit and commune with Him—to be still and rest—is because we are moving at such a fast pace. If our thoughts are constantly going, then He can't get a word in. The soul is so LOUD! The Lord has to dial our minds down so that our spirit can rise up and hear. God wants to put His thoughts in between our thoughts. I pray as you become still in Him today and commune with Him, clarity comes with insight, understanding, direction, and revelation. May He give you strategy keys today that you need in this season!

I learned when you make life about knowing Him; you position yourself in a place for Him to reveal dreams, visions, and ideas that He has for your destiny. When I began to dwell in that place with Him, His creativity started to flow through me, and things were birthed in me. The same will happen for you.

THE POWER OF THE SECRET PLACE

It is in that place that you truly capture some things. For what you are able to capture in the secret place, you are able to display in public. The Lord ministered to me; it's what you do in private that determines the anointing you carry in public. Ministry is birthed in the secret place with Him, and as you minister to Him, He ministers back to you. There is an exchange of life with the creator Himself, in which His thoughts and ideas are awakened in you. What is revealed to you, you then become a carrier of and you minister it out. But, it all starts in that intimate place and abiding in Him.

Jesus said in John 15:7, "If you abide in Me and My words abide in you, (take up residence in you, colonize in you, live in your heart), you will ask what you will and it shall be done unto you. Here in is My Father glorified that you bear MUCH FRUIT!" (Emphasis mine.)

You may be trying to bear fruit without abiding in Him and abiding in the place where He has set you - in the place where He has planted you. Set means to abide, to continue, to dwell.

No abiding means no anointing, which in turn means, no fruit. However, if you will spend time with Him in the secret place and abide in Him, you will ABOUND!

Are you looking for answers in your life? If you will abide in the vine and get into His Word, you will receive wisdom and revelation on the matter at hand. It is the power of the Spirit of God that will bring answers to your situation, and bring change in areas of your life. Ask the Holy Spirit to illuminate the Word of God and cause it to come alive in you. For it is then that you will walk in the light of the Word and receive a fresh anointing.

Through Intimacy with Him Comes an Anointing
Intimacy produces the presence and glory of God. The true Presence will produce a true Anointing—tangible, feel-able, know-able, substance—a precious commodity we call the anointing. As you spend time in the secret place with the Holy Spirit and abide in Him, a greater anointing comes upon your life for His purposes. There is an anointing within us (1 John 2:27), and there is an anointing that comes upon us for service.

We have not been trained in His abiding presence, nor how to minister with Him, empowered by Him, and imparting Him to others. We need to shift our attention to the presence of the Holy Spirit that has been given to us because everything revolves around our intimate relationship with Him. The more time I spend with Him, the more I know Him.

I love when God sends me out on little assignments. I have had many assignments through the years—at the nail salon, hair salon, the spa, the mall, you name it. God wants to use you everywhere you go if you will allow Him to.

We need to realize that as we go places, Holy Spirit is actually coming upon us in power that we might impart Him to others. We have been sent to invade the area that has been occupied by the enemy, and take back that territory for the Kingdom. We are carriers of His presence, and we are to release Him into the environment whether we are in ministry or whether we work a vocational job.

THE NAIL SALON

One particular day, I was riding my friend's bike to the beach in California. While riding, I passed a nail salon, and as I did, I heard the Holy Spirit say, "Turn around, go in there and get your nails done." I didn't particularly want to get my nails done that day, but I was compelled and drawn by love to go. As I walked in, I noticed I was the only customer in the salon. An asian woman came up to me and said, "Can I help you?" I said, "Yes, I'd like to get my nails done."

As we sat down, I looked around, and I noticed a Buddha statue, so I assumed she was Buddhist. As we visited, the Lord gave me a word of knowledge for her concerning her family.

As I shared the word, she began to tear up and said, "How did you know that?" I told her Jesus Christ loves her so much that He sent me in there to speak to her and tell her how much He loves her. She then broke down and cried.

The anointing became strong on me, and I laid my hands on her to release healing into her body. She had battled pain in her shoulder for years as well as migraines. As soon as I laid hands on her and prayed, all the pain left her body immediately. She was amazed! I shared the Gospel with her afterward and she accepted Jesus as her Lord and Savior. Glory to God! He is always looking for vessels to use if we will just make ourselves available.

We need God's presence and anointing to accomplish the tasks and challenges that are at hand. The anointing will not only destroy every yoke of bondage that is hard for you (due to the conformity of the world), but it will also bring a supply of the Spirit that makes it effortless for you to do certain things that you have always wanted to do.

I have learned you can't win yesterday's battles on yesterday's anointing. You need a fresh anointing for each day. I ask God daily for a fresh anointing on my life to do everything He has called me to do that day. I believe if you ask Him, He will release a fresh anointing on your life. You have not because you ask not. So ask! With a fresh anointing, you will be able to go where you've never been and accomplish what you could never do in the natural.

God is calling you to that intimate secret place with Him. He is calling you to an ever-deepening, inward walk and talk with Him. There are things He desires to show you and birth in you in this season. In that place, you will see and know some things, and greater growth will come. He designed the inward man to constantly grow as you live a lifestyle of walking with Him.

New seasons and divine doors will open to those who are going somewhere on the inside. Purpose to get in that place where your heart and head are aligned and engaged in His Word. It will bring increase, wisdom, and insight to your inward man. Then you will be ready to walk through the divine doors of purpose He opens for you.

It's in YOU!

CHAPTER TWO

TRUE IDENTITY

Have you ever lost something precious? I recall a time when I was taking care of my niece; she was only about three at the time. We were playing upstairs together when I needed to run downstairs to get something; it would only take a minute. I was going to take her downstairs with me, but she was having so much fun I decided to let her play. I thought surely; she'll be alright. I mean, what could she do in a minute or two? Where could she go?

I ran downstairs to get what I needed, and when I came back up, she was nowhere to be found. We had been playing hide and seek earlier, so I thought, maybe she was hiding in one of the girl's rooms. I began looking in the other bedrooms, under the beds, in the closets and frantically calling out her name. But, I couldn't find her. My heart was pounding and racing. I felt like

I was about to have a panic attack. The upstairs had two sets of stairs at the opposite ends of the house.

Before I ran down the stairs on the other side, the Spirit of God quickened me to commission my angels to find her. I prayed and commissioned my angels to find Sierra and bring her back to me. I ran down the stairs into the living room, and there she was walking back into the house through the back door. In that short period of time, she made her way down the stairs and out the door.

LOSING YOUR IDENTITY

After I processed what had just happened, I thought about what it felt like to lose something that is so dear and so precious to us, even if it's just for a moment. Then, I thought about how often we lose—perhaps for a very long time—our self through a tragedy in our life. We lose our true identity, which is something that is most valuable to us.

When you don't know who you are, and you lose yourself, you'll live a false life. You'll live a life that pleases everyone but yourself. You will live a life that strives to gain acceptance from people who don't care. When you live that kind of life, it means you have lost yourself. You've lost your purpose in life; you're uncertain what God has called you to. If you lose yourself, it is very difficult to have an intimate relationship with God. The enemy constantly works to destroy your relationship with God. He wants to rob you of your destiny, and so his purpose is to confuse you of your identity.

My question to you is: Do you know your true identity and who you are? If you don't know who you are, you can't embrace who other people are in your life, and who God is in your life. The question is: How do I live out of my identity and my purpose? How do I discover my purpose and discover who I really am?

Let's explore what the Word of God tells us about our identity.

> *"For as many as are led by the Spirit of God, they are the sons of God. For ye have not received the spirit of bondage again to fear; but ye have received the Spirit of adoption, whereby we cry, Abba, Father. The Spirit itself bears witness with our spirit that we are the children of God. And if children, then heirs; heirs of God, and joint-heirs with Christ; if so be that we suffer with him, that we may be also glorified together."* ROMANS 8:14-17 (KJV)

The Holy Spirit will always bear witness to the spirit of a person. You are a spirit, you have a soul, and you live in a body. You have a spirit in you where the Holy Spirit dwells. That is where the Holy Spirit communicates to your spirit that you are a child of God.

You are an heir of God, joint heirs with Christ Jesus. What does that really mean? It is a revelation that is still being revealed (or coming to light). Holy Spirit makes groanings for us that cannot be uttered. His target is to reveal who you are. The earth is groaning, and the Holy Spirit is groaning in intercession for you and me to know who we really are.

"Who is he that condemneth? It is Christ that dies, yea rather, that is risen again, who is even at the right hand of God, who also maketh intercession for us."

ROM. 8:34 (KJV)

Now we have creation, the Spirit, and the Son of God all groaning with one thing in mind; for you and me to know who we are. It is not self-identity and self-achievement, he wants to reveal the significant of adoption that He chose you and me. He chose us when we were dead in our sins and had no options. It was His redemptive power in our lives that purchased us and brought us into a family with eternal significance that will carry on throughout eternity.

All this intercession takes place so that we can discover who we are in Christ. Our identity is found in Him. Jesus has paid the price for us to know our significance and who we are in Him. His desire is for you to know the purpose He has called you to while you are here on earth.

The day you were born, you had all the inherit strength, goodness, and wisdom that you will ever need. All there was to gain was your knowledge to access it. Everything you need in your life is deposited on the inside of you. Your specific purpose is within you— it's inherited. You need the wisdom of God through his Word, to come into alignment with the decree and the decisions God has already made about you.

THROUGH THE VALLEY

Job 22:29 in the Message Bible says, "To those who feel low you'll say, 'Chin up! Be brave!' and God will save them." It's in the low places, the valley, that we can often miss out on destiny. Sometimes it's in the transitions that we tend to get confused. Many times, we don't understand how the valley can be used for any purpose at all. Often, however, those valleys will become the springboard to the higher places, the mountaintops.

If you find yourself in the valley right now, raise your chin up and be encouraged because that valley does not determine or define your destiny. But God will use it for your good by doing deep work in you – to prepare you to step into the next season. The valley is a place where everything about you dies and Christ lives. Often, it is synonymous with what many call the wilderness season. Jesus went through a wilderness season before He was launched into His ministry. It is in this season where character and steadfastness are forged.

One of the greatest blessings in my life is that God has delivered me from me, and continues to perfect that in my life. He has reduced me to Christ, for "I have been crucified with Christ; it is no longer I who live, but Christ lives in me" (Gal. 2:20). In this position, you have no fear of what people think; you don't care about your image or your reputation, or that you are, or are not, politically correct, but it is in Christ. We may not have completely arrived at this position, but we are well on our way. It is in Him that we live, move, and have our being. This is a place where people don't move you because you are spirit led. Therefore, it's a place where God can really use you.

Many times, our greatest joys come from challenging and even crisis situations. Often, they reveal what you are called to do. Who we are and our depth of growth as a person will be revealed in times of conflict and crisis. I have found it is when we are under pressure that we find out what is on the inside of us. I often say, challenges do not make you who you are, they reveal who you are.

It is easy to live your best life when things are going smoothly and when everything is going your way. But, how you handle life's disappointments and mishaps when things become difficult and rocky reveal your authentic character.

> *"Therefore, whoever hears these sayings of Mine, and does them, I will liken him to a wise man who built his house on the rock: and the rain descended, the floods came, and the winds blew and beat on that house; and it did not fall, for it was founded on the rock. But everyone who hears these sayings of Mine, and does not do them, will be like a foolish man who built his house on the sand: and the rain descended, the floods came, and the winds blew and beat on that house, and it fell. And great was its fall."*

> MATT. 7:24-27 (KJV)

Jesus clearly says that you will not be able to avoid life and its ebbs and flows. There will be rough waters, jagged edges, and zigzags on your journey. You will get thrown many curve balls from out of left field. But, do not let that detour you, or hold you back. Value your life and the moment you're in now because time is moving on. God has called you on an assignment to be an influencer and a game-changer in this world today.

Walking and being in the spirit is a direction we take as opposed to a destination we reach. We are to live our lives by living in the spirit—to live in purpose daily, and to live a life of purpose. This is a decision we make. "I say then: Walk in the Spirit, and you shall not fulfill the lust of the flesh" (Gal. 5:16). The word walk in the Greek means to follow or tread around.

In Jesus' parable about the house on the rock, we see that the size of the storm is not what holds the most significance. We all go through "storms" in our lives. The real significance, He says, is in the substance of the foundation. Therefore, Jesus went on to say that every person who hears His words and puts them into practice, builds a strong foundation.

If you hear the Word, and you know you were called to live a life of purpose, to become a game-changer, and to bring heaven to earth, but you do not practice these concepts, then you are building on a faulty foundation. If the foundation is faulty, when life hits you, it will all come crashing down. If you practice the Word of God in your life, and activate your faith, then you are building a firm, solid foundation that is immovable and unshakable.

PARTICIPATOR OR SPECTATOR?

Jesus said there are two categories into which people will fall— participators or spectators. Participators are those who hear and practice His Word; they are doers of the Word. They build on The Rock, and they have a firm foundation. Spectators, on the other hand, are those who hear His word, but do not practice His Word, and fail to take action. They are foolish, and they build on shifting sand, which will fail in the time of the storms. We get out of the valleys in life by being a participator and building our life on the Word of God and putting it into practice. We do not just hear the Word, but we become a doer of the Word.

You were called with a purpose to be the difference; it is up to you to decide when you are going to become a participator and make a difference. If not now, then when? How long has God been urging you to move out and take action? Perhaps, He wants you to start a business, or He is urging you to preach His Gospel to the world, or maybe He wants you to write a book or a blog. In order to come up higher into a greater place of fulfillment that God has for you, you have to put the Word of God into practice. You must take action.

It is time to adopt God's mindset. God lives in the realm of possibilities, and that is where He wants you and me to live. He has revelation with no limitation, and we have access to that. Revelation removes the veil from something that has been hidden. It's an impartation of revelation that really changes a person and reveals who they are. Revelation is based on how God sees things, not how we see things. So when we get a revelation about something, we can see with our spiritual eyes the way God sees. It allows us to see ourselves the way God sees us. God sees things completely different than the way man sees things.

Man may try to disqualify you, but God will qualify you every time. Your job is come into alignment and agree with the decree of God. God's purpose and plan will not be disqualified by man's opinion. People may say you can't do this or you can't do that because of certain things that happened in your life. But, God has the final say.

CHOICE, NOT CHANCE

We must develop a mindset and way of thinking that always puts God into our circumstances. "But we have the mind of Christ, the Messiah, and do hold the thoughts, feelings, and purposes of His heart" (1 Cor. 2:16). You can choose to build strength or live in your weaknesses. Life is all about choice, not about chance. Putting God's Word into practice is a choice that we make. It takes effort and discipline; every day we make a choice to apply the Word of God to our situation. We may not feel like it—most likely we won't feel like it—but we choose it anyway. It is a discipline and a decision we make that we will cut away everything in our life that contradicts what God says.

We have to cut away every thought and cast down every imagination. We have the choice to think on these things, whatsoever is honest, just, pure, lovely and of good report (Phil. 4:8). It is important to make a course correction where your thoughts move away from anything that disagrees with God's thoughts.

The mind is the place of all spiritual and carnal conflict. In other words, there will be a constant battle in our minds between flesh and between the spirit. The carnal mind means to have the nature of the flesh, which is sensual and controlled by the five senses. The spiritual mind is a mind that is controlled by the Spirit of God. This is a choice that we make, and it needs to become a lifestyle in our life to live victoriously.

FAITH BASED ON GOD'S WORD

Faith is based on the knowledge of God's Word and God's character. That is how faith arises in our hearts. Faith is based on the fact that God's Word will never fail. God is the same yesterday, today, and forever.

We cannot produce faith. Faith is what God's Word produces on the inside of us. In essence, faith is the persuasion of a mind that a statement or idea is true and worthy of trust. Therefore, if God said it, it is settled. We have to reframe our life to be a student of God's Word and not a victim of life's circumstances.

WHAT DEFINES YOU?

An event does not define you. Your past experiences, do not determine who you are. Just because something happened to you, or because of you, it is not the end. Your past does not determine your future. Everyone in life will have situations and circumstances that contradict who they really are. Many have dysfunctional parents or families. Perhaps you have encountered fragile people who are flawed and hurting. Just because you grew up in a dysfunctional atmosphere, doesn't mean you can't soar like an eagle.

I challenge you to reconsider the way you see yourself and to reframe your understanding of who you are and why you are here.

No matter how you see yourself or what you have gone through in life, there is a great purpose for you. Make the decision today to take the Word of God that says you can live an abundant life - a life that is superior in quality. Get in the game and stay focused because He has a greater plan for you. It's about the bigger plan—God's plan! It's time for you to step into your true identity and begin to live life on purpose.

It's in YOU!

CHAPTER THREE

AUTHENTIC YOU

As a young woman in my early twenties, I was enraptured by the stories my grandparents and other family members would share, as they gathered on special occasions. I listened intently as they would tell stories and share experiences of their own childhoods. I was captivated and became a sponge, soaking up everything I could. I saw that these stories contained wisdom, family values, and even revealed their authentic selves. These stories were a powerful tool that communicated their unique experiences and beliefs; the essence of who they were. They became a vehicle for me to look at my life and ask God who am I and who have You made me to be.

Living authentically takes courage and conviction. It requires self-love. Otherwise, we will never have the courage to step out in our unique gifts and be who we really are. It also involves a willingness to be vulnerable and be real. Far too many of us are wearing a mask of who or what we are expected to be because of the fear of rejection.

God loves you and will never reject who you are. Who you are in Him, and your position in Him never changes. This means you can line up with who you are authentically because behavior comes out of a belief. When you know who you are, you, will stop doing things that are contrary to the Word of God—things that are not in alignment with your authentic self. When you know whose you are, you will walk in the freedom to be YOU!

Authenticity is highly being sought out today. People want the real deal. People are looking for authentic. They seek true authenticity, but what does being authentic mean? A relevant definition would be, "you know it when you see it." The dictionary defines authentic as, genuine, real, true, trustworthy, honest, pure, not fake and phony.

Young people are especially hungry for the real deal. They are searching for it. They have the uncanny ability to identify phoniness immediately and see right through the fakeness of a person. As soon as they identify the phoniness, they walk away. They're not interested.

People are looking for the real person. They are not interested in imposters who look and speak the part, while they are hiding their true identity behind a mask. I believe people want to trust that they are getting what they see.

Many times, when you come up against a fake and phony person, you're not sure what it is that you're sensing, but something's not quite right. If you ask the Spirit of God to reveal truth to you, He will. The Bible says in John 16:13 (NKJV): "However, when He, the Spirit of truth, has come, He will guide you into all truth; for He will not speak on His authority, but whatever He hears He will speak; and He will tell you things to come."

Being authentic is being real. Real is something you can see. There is a visible difference between real and fake. It is not enough to say you are real; others should be able to see you are real. Being real runs deep. People are looking for men and women who are true to their word. They want to know that they are a man or a woman of their word, people who do what they say they are going to do.

If you are real, it will reveal itself in your life and how you lead people – whether in business, education, or ministry. Your authenticity will be revealed in ways that can be seen, heard, and felt. It will exemplify true sincerity of the heart.

The younger generation loves authenticity and transparency. They don't want to see religion and religious rituals. They want something that is genuine and authentic. They want something that comes from the heart and says, "Be real with me. Do not give me a bunch of dos and don'ts that people cannot live by. But, be authentic with me and tell me when you messed up and need the grace of God in your own life." When we can be honest and tell people the truth that our failures have taught us more than our successes ever will, that is what really helps them because it comes from the heart.

What comes from the heart goes to the heart. When we

speak from our heart, God speaks to the heart. The Spirit of God begins to pierce a person, and He speaks and touches their heart. It is a heart to heart connection.

NOT CALLED TO BE PERFECT

We are not called to be perfect. I believe God desires for us to have a spirit of excellence about us in all that we do, but we do not have to be concerned about being perfect all the time—never making a mistake or never experiencing failure. I do not believe people are looking for us to be perfect. People are looking for someone they can respect, someone who is real, authentic, and who truly cares.

People do not care how much you know until they know how much you care. To be an influential voice and make an impact in the body of Christ and to unbelievers, we must be authentic. Without authenticity, there is no real connection with people. People want you to be you, not someone else. God wants you to be you, not imitate somebody else. Most often, it seems there is a risk in that because it requires you to step into a place of vulnerability. You have to step into a place that reveals more of your heart, your style, and your ideas, and that, in turn, opens you up to possible rejection. However, it is in that place where the authentic you comes out and has an opportunity to make a greater impact on peoples lives. You were born to be an original, not a copy. Go where you are celebrated and not tolerated. Be YOU!

TRUE AUTHENTICITY

Authenticity means transparency; alignment to what is. I would say it is matching the outer expression with inner experience. The word authentic comes from the Latin word authenticus meaning "coming from the author." God authors our lives and makes us authentic. You are an original! God created only one YOU. He deposited certain things in you to do the impossible and achieve the unbelievable. David tells us in Psalm 139:14-16 that we are fearfully and wonderfully made. It says,

"I will praise You, for I am fearfully and wonderfully made; Marvelous are Your works, And that my soul knows very well. My frame was not hidden from You, When I was made in secret, And skillfully wrought in the lowest parts of the earth. Your eyes saw my substance, being yet unformed. And in Your book they all were written, The days fashioned for me when as yet there were none of them.

God values you, and He values you being you. He created you in uniqueness, and He desires for you to walk in that uniqueness in Christ.

There are times we all have felt uncomfortable with our own skills and abilities, so we tried to be someone else. If you allow yourself to hide behind a mask, then you stand to lose trust, intimacy, and your own sense of integrity. But, if you remove the mask and are willing to be authentic, it not only liberates you—it touches and inspires people around you.

God desires for us to tap into who He has created us to be.

He wants us to tap into our thoughts and our expressions that He has deposited on the inside of us individually. He wants us to be comfortable and confident in who He created us to be and operate out of that authentic place. In that place is where the anointing flows. God anoints authenticity!

MENTORS

Mentors are inspiring, and I believe an essential part of our development. They help us come into who we are. It is important to serve someone who in return becomes a mentor in your life for you to learn and glean from. You should seek God about serving someone — ask Him who He would desire for you to serve and glean from.

There was a time when I was seeking God asking Him who He wanted me to serve because I needed wisdom and a lot of it. I needed it to go where I knew the Lord wanted to take me in my destiny. I knew in my heart there was a woman He wanted me to glean and receive from, but I didn't know who. One Sunday morning, I came across a woman that was unlike any other woman I had ever met, something about her intrigued me. God was on her! She came walking down the hallway and our paths crossed for the first time. When I looked into her eyes, I saw life that spoke back to me without ever saying a word, and I knew immediately we were of the same spirit. We spoke briefly, but when she spoke, it left me wanting to know more of what she had to say. I did not know who she was. But, I knew I had to get to know her and spend some time with her, but I didn't know how.

At that moment, up from my spirit came a principle I was reminded of– Everybody, no matter how much money or things they have always has a need in their life. So, I began to inquire of the Lord as to how I could get to know this woman and spend some time with her. I said, "Lord, show me a need in this woman's life that I can meet." Immediately, He showed me something which was a way to serve her to meet a need, and it opened an amazing door for this woman and I to not only become friends but to experience this beautiful mother/daughter relationship. She became a mentor to me and began to pour wisdom into me in all areas of life, and still does. She became my pastor, my mentor, and a mother to me. As I asked the Lord to show me a need she had, it opened up an immediate door to serve, which has led to years of a beautiful relationship of gleaning and receiving from her.

This kind of serving is what Ruth did to Boaz. She went to his feet. First, she was a wise woman that knew how to receive instruction from a wiser woman of God who was like a mother to her. She followed her instructions and went to Boaz's feet. Feet are emblematic of needs. Ruth went to him, uncovered his feet and laid at his feet. To uncover the feet means to discover a person's needs and meet them. Ruth uncovered Boaz's feet then discovered the need and met the need. It caused him to notice her.

If you want to influence a person's heart, serve them. There is no better way to connect with a person's heart than to serve them. It will cause your heart to be connected with them. As you serve someone, they will begin to open the treasure of their life and download wisdom into you just because you serve them. They will talk to you and pour wisdom into you like a mother talking to her daughter or a father talking to his son. This wisdom cannot be bought. It's priceless!

God is brilliant at aligning us with the right person that fits our uniqueness. God is into the details, and He knows every little detail about us. He knows how to connect us with someone that not only loves what we love but someone that will challenge us, sharpen us and even hold our feet to the fire, if need be. He will connect us to someone who will relate to who we are, without us pretending to be someone we're not. Someone who will allow us to be our authentic self, and will invest in us to help polish and refine us. The reason they invest in you is because they see themselves in you and they are trying to pull you up to the next level that you desire to go. They pour into you because they believe in your potential.

The right mentor will have a generous spirit towards you. They will want you to succeed, and will actively support your success with their words and actions. Great mentors will never be envious or feel threatened by someone's growth, but they will celebrate them and help them recover from any setbacks. The right mentor will make connections for you when the time is right and offer resources outside of themselves that may be useful. Great mentors pour their lives into people and support them to become the person they desire to be. God anoints them to know just how to speak into your life to provoke you and bring correction without crushing your spirit. He uses them so intricately to help guide you to the next level of your destiny. Their impact in your life is not only life-changing, but it's also empowering you for the more that God has for you.

EXPLORING NEW TERRITORIES

New adventures with God means exploring new territories, not only on the outside but on the inside. We often look to a mentor and even others to see how they do things—how they flow and operate. We try to imitate people we admire. It's okay to do that for a while because it will give you a chance to practice certain skills. It becomes a tool to help you grow so that you can integrate them into your personality.

Once you become comfortable and confident, you will be skillful with your own style. Then, you quickly shift from trying to be someone else, to doing things well like someone you admire. I believe that is a tool the Lord uses to help us walk in excellence in all our endeavors. Once we begin to use our signature voice and giftings, the more effective we will be in connecting with others and getting results. (More about your signature voice in a later chapter.)

BE TRUE TO WHO YOU ARE

Staying true to who you are is paramount as you journey through life. The Bible tells us about a man who was sent from God, whose name was John. He came as a witness to testify about the Light. He was not the light, but he came to testify about the Light (John 1:6-8). In other words, John said, "I'm not the light, but my job is to testify and point you to the Light."

Some people have to come to an understanding that they are not the light. John is happy being who he is and doing what he is called to do. Many people are frustrated trying to be someone they're not. Their reason is that they are trying to find ways to be recognized and acknowledged in what they think is prestigious. So, they stop being John and they try to be Jesus, metaphorically speaking.

John knew he was not the light, but he was good at pointing to the One who was The Light. He was true to his purpose and giftings. Do what you know you are good at? What you're good at will reveal to you what your purpose is. The level of your gifting will reveal to you the level of your destiny. God will give you the gifting for what you are called to do. If you don't have the gifting and are not good in a particular area, don't try to force it and do it anyway.

Many people don't know what they are called to do. They don't know their purpose in life—they don't know their skill set. When you look at what you're good at, you will know your skill set, and then you will know what you are called to do. God will give you skills according to what He predestined you for. If He gave you the skills and giftings to be John, then do that one message—that one purpose and point people to Jesus. You will receive the same "well done good and faithful servant," as those who had more because you give account only for the level of giftings you have.

We must find where we fit and be authentic. John wasn't sent here to redeem the world; he was sent to bear witness to the light. We will never know what we're sent to do until we know what we're not sent to do. Many times we get forced into areas where we don't fit because people put us there. Other times, we mimic someone else because we don't know who we are yet.

Being authentic means being true to who you are, not someone else. It also means being skillful, yet flexible enough to yield to the Spirit of God; to let go, step into the unknown and allow Him to flow through you the way He desires to. It means being skillful, knowledgeable, and disciplined as a way to connect with people so He can flow through you more effectively. It also means caring enough about the people you are with to let the walls down and open your heart.

ALL AUTHENTIC MINISTRY FLOWS OUT OF GOD'S PRESENCE

As a minister of the Gospel, it is important that I minister with an authenticity about me. I have learned to open my heart and be more transparent so that people can really connect and receive from God. That is not always easy to do because you guard yourself to keep from getting hurt. If I'm not real with them, showing them that I'm a real person who has had or may still have difficult issues in my life then they will look at me as perfect and say, "I can't achieve that, I might as well not even try."

Whatever vocation we're in, especially ministry, it is important that we carry ourselves with authenticity. We should honor the anointing and be mindful to weigh our words before speaking. Words have power. Marketing companies know words have power. Historians know words have power. Words have the power to shape a nation. Martin Luther King knew that words have power. I can't help but get chills throughout my body every time I hear him say, "I have a dream."

Most people can remember a time when a schoolteacher who commanded something about them, or a coach who told them to stick with it because they could do it, or a youth pastor who spoke encouragement to them right when they needed it. With these encouraging words, they felt they possessed the means to accomplish the task. I can remember times when my dad spoke words to me that gave me encouragement when my courage was faltering. The words he spoke to me, strengthened me to press on, or the words my mentor spoke to me, that not only strengthened and empowered me but settled me and released peace over me in times of uneasiness and difficulty.

WORDS HAVE POWER

We know that words have power, and the absence of words can be devastating in people's lives. Perhaps in your own life, you never heard words of affirmation or encouragement. For many people growing up, the only words they remember from their parents were such words as, "You'll never amount to anything." Or they may have been labeled with names like stupid.

Words deeply imprint us. All children have a deep yearning to hear words of delight from their parents. Throughout our lives, I do not believe we ever tire of hearing words of affirmation. They are an essential part, not only in our continual development and growth but in our achievements and fulfilling our destiny.

As believers, God has entrusted us to speak healing words of life and wholeness to people. We get to say words such as, "You have a loving Father, and He values you greatly. You matter to your Creator. He loves you, and He's crazy about you. Jesus came to save you and restore you to your Father." We not only get to say these words, but we get to see the impact in their lives as tears roll down their faces as they hear these words their heart longs to hear. The authenticity flows as our heart connects with God for that person.

DAVID'S CONFIDENCE IN WHO HE WAS IN GOD

How many times have you tried to be another person and God just wanted you to be you? David knew there was power in humility and authenticity. He knew there would be an anointing on the real him, not someone he was trying to be. The real anointing is always on the real you. God only anoints the authentic self. I believe the more confident we are in Him, the more authentic we will become.

David put his confidence in his God. We see a particular incident in David's life right before he fought Goliath. In 1 Sam. 17:38-39 we read:

"So, Saul clothed David with his armor, and he put a bronze helmet on his head; he also clothed him with a coat of mail. David fastened his sword to his armor and tried to walk, for he had not tested them. And David said to Saul, "I cannot walk with these, for I have not tested them." So David took them off."

Out of respect for Saul, David attempted to walk around in his armor. But, he made a decision that he couldn't wear what someone else wore to battle because it was not custom-tailored for him. He could not put his confidence in Saul's armor. He had to put his confidence in what God had custom-tailored for him.

Confidence doesn't just enable you to put stuff on; it also empowers you to know what to take off—what doesn't fit for you. It was almost as if David was saying, "The way I do it may not be impressive to you; it may not be the way that you would do it; but if you give me my rocks and my slingshot and let me do it the way God designed me to do it, this giant will come down."

Unknowingly, David had been conditioned by God to have

that kind of confidence and authenticity. David's confidence and authenticity were being cultivated even in his selection as king. God sent Samuel to Jesse's house to look for a king. 1 Sam. 16:1 says, "Fill your horn with oil, and go; I am sending you to Jesse the Bethlehemite. For I have provided Myself a king among his sons."

Samuel obeyed the Lord. When he arrived, he consecrated Jesse and his sons for the sacrifice. Jesse, who is David's father, had seven of his sons pass before Samuel, but he never called for David. All this time, Jesse had a king in his house, and he didn't even know it. (Sometimes the people who think they know you the best, know you the least.)

Seven of Jesse's sons pass before David. Then Samuel said to Jesse, "Are all the young men here?" Then he said, "There remains yet the youngest, and there he is, keeping the sheep." (1 Sam. 16:11)

Jesse did not call for David because he did not think David looked the part. But, Samuel said, "Send and bring him. For we will not sit down till he comes here." When David walked in front of Samuel, he may not have met Jesse's criteria, but he certainly met God's criteria. God's criteria is always a heart criterion.

"Do not look at his appearance or his physical stature, because I have refused him. For the Lord does not see as man sees; for man looks at the outward appearance, but the Lord looks at the heart."   I SAM. 16:7

41

David walked in front of Samuel, and God spoke and said, " Arise, anoint him; for this is the one!"

This is amazing. Seven people went in front of the ram's horn before David did and the oil never flowed. But when David arrived, the oil began to flow. That tells me that when God has something for you, it doesn't matter who has gone before you, He will hold it in place until you get there!

When you know who you are, and who you belong to, you will not be intimidated by others. You will live confidently in who God has made you to be—that you are unique, and equipped with special giftings and creativity. Confidence will allow you to sit in the back, wait your turn, and not be anxious. You have a knowing in your heart that what God has for you He has only for you. He will bring you from the back to the front. He will bring you out of hiding and into prominence.

Many times, we try to manipulate our way with people and circumstances so we can obtain what we think God has promised us. He may have indeed promised us something, but He will give it to us in His time, not ours. He will open all the doors we need to be opened if we listen to His voice and follow His leading.

Samuel anointed David in the presence of his brothers. The same brothers who didn't believe in him had to watch the oil they wanted to be administered to another. God will bless you in front of your enemies in spite of what they did to stop it.

David carried the difference on the inside, and he knew it. He had a covenant, and the brothers did not. On the outside,

David did not look like he had much to offer, but on the inside, he carried what made all the difference.

Like David, when you are a child of God, you carry the difference on the inside. It's in you because God has put it there. He has anointed you and placed His confidence in you. Your part is to believe it, honor it and use it!

COMPARISON—THE ENEMY'S STRATEGY

God is a strategic God, and He has marked out a path for us to run individually that is unique in its design for our life. He made us be an original. Therefore, you are not "just" anything. You are God's representative in whatever vocation you're in. You are strategically placed there for His purposes.

The challenge of life, year after year, is to stay where God has placed us; to run our race and not compare ourselves to others. We are to fix our eyes on Him and stay our course. The day we start running our race with our eyes focused on what others are doing, is the day things will begin to look confused, foggy, out of sorts, and we will eventually crash.

Comparing is what caused Saul to shift his attention and subsequently fall. He compared himself to David. He shifted his focus and attention to what David was doing.

Saul was anointed and appointed by God to be the first king of Israel. The Bible says Saul looked like a king. He stood head-and-shoulders above any other person. God placed him in that position and blessed him.

We have to steward the blessing of God. If we don't steward the blessing that God brings into our lives, we will lose it. Saul became blinded to what God had done in his life. So much so that he was more concerned about being the king instead of worshiping the King of kings. He was more concerned about keeping his position than he was hungering for God's presence. God eventually removed him from his position as king and replaced him with a man after His heart.

David had a heart for God. He didn't care about a title or position. All David cared about was worshiping His God and being in His presence. One day David was faced with great opposition, which turned out to be a great opportunity in disguise. He took his place and defeated Goliath in the name of the Lord. The moment Goliath fell to the ground, David was immediately elevated to a new position. That moment of opposition was a destiny moment for David.

Not all moments are created equal. There are some destiny moments that bring a shift and everything changes in an instant. In a moment, David's life was changed, and he was catapulted out of obscurity and into notoriety. I pray that you will come into a destiny moment where the trajectory of your life changes suddenly! Get ready, because promotion from God comes quick. You don't have time to play around or be concerned about what others may think of you. In a moment, everybody knew David's name, and he was elevated to a position of authority.

David didn't compare himself to others. He walked in who he was and kept his eyes fixed on his God. Saul, on the other hand, focused his eyes on David. He could not separate his life and successes from David's. When Saul heard about all the praise David was getting from killing Goliath he said, "They have credited David with tens of thousands, but me with only thousands" (1 Sam. 18:8). Saul was comparing himself to David.

Comparison will always lead us to the end of something. It will cause us to become jealous and envious—it will even rob us of our joy and peace. It will cause us to focus on ourselves to where we see everything in life through the lens of "me". The focus of our life is not supposed to be on us. We are to fix our eyes on Jesus; then we can do what He has called us to do.

The weight of intimidation will fall on us when we compare ourselves with others (how they run their race), to the way God has called us to run our race. Comparison will hold us back from walking in the fulfillment of our destiny. Don't let that happen to you! Shake off every weight of comparison and rest in God's truth that He has given you grace for your race. He has graced you to be you and run your race in confidence. He has been training and developing you for a specific assignment. God wants to move you into that in this season. It's time for you to step into it! Be you—be authentic!

It's in YOU!

CHAPTER FOUR

SIGNIFICANCE

I have always been a goal setter and have stretched myself to attain more. I remember when I ran my first marathon. Through all the hard work, sweat, and time invested, I felt such a sense of accomplishment. I experienced a thrill crossing that finish line. I had overcome many challenges to get to that point.

The week before the marathon, I twisted my ankle badly but was determined to run the marathon even with the swelling and pain. At the outset, I did not know if I had it in me to run 26.2 miles, especially now that my ankle was compromised. I wanted to be able to finish it and cross the finish line, but I was uncertain because I had never run a marathon before.

I started out strong, but as I began to approach the seventeenth mile, my body hit a wall. The struggle was real. Every step felt like I was barely making it. My body was screaming at me to stop, but as I began to quote scripture and ask the Lord to renew my strength to finish the race, I discovered a greater strength and tenacity on the inside of me. I finished that race in a greater time than I expected and what a thrill that was!

I have learned that challenges don't make you who you are, they reveal who you are. There have been other times in my life that I have not only come up against some very challenging situations but devastating situations. It was in those times, once again, that I discovered what was inside of me, along with some things that were lacking in me that I needed.

LOOK WITHIN YOURSELF

There are times in our lives that we encounter an exciting joy, or perhaps even a devastating situation. In either instance, it seems the world around us comes to a halt, and we are forced to look within ourselves. It's at that point that we discover what's really inside of us. We discover what is at the very core of our being.

At that point, it's not about what we say we believe; it is about what we truly believe about who we are, who God is, and what life is all about. It is in those moments that we realize what we are made of. It is in those moments that you discover what you have been feeding on, and what you have been putting in your spirit, because, rest assured, it will come out.

These moments in our lives trigger many emotions. You may find yourself feeling powerful, excited, joyful, energized, inspired, and exhilarated about life. However, you may find yourself powerless, fearful, uncertain, and defeated. Emotions can be a tricky thing. They will lie to you and get you all worked up, with the purpose of putting you into a whirlwind spin. I'm so thankful we have the Word of God to stand on. We can believe the truth of God's word, instead of being tossed to and fro with our emotions.

THE IMPORTANT QUESTION

Whatever situation you find yourself in—whether it's full of opportunity and purpose, or a fearful storm, we all want to know: Do I have what it takes within me to make it through this?

Whether you're aware of it or not, how you answer this question carries life-changing significance for you and the people around you. It plays a big role in how you see yourself and how others see you. The direction of your life will be determined by what actions you take, depending on how you answer this question. How you answer the question can either focus your attention on God's supernatural power and His supply of provision within you, or it will cause you to focus on your limitations.

Life will always present new challenges and new mountains to climb. As we grow in our faith by experiencing God's faithfulness and goodness in our lives, we become more confident in Him-in-us and the fullness of His ability through us.

I have learned that God likes to interest us in extraordinary, life-changing opportunities. He will present to us life-changing invitations which, in turn, will cause us to discover more of what

God has deposited inside of us.

NEW TERRITORY; NEW SEASON

I recall one Sunday when I experienced an invitation from God for a new opportunity. It started Sunday evening during a church service; God shifted some things in my life. That morning I ministered to a little church in Missouri. It was a wonderful service; several people got saved while many received healing in their bodies. There was such an excitement in the house that we were all looking forward to the evening service. That night in the service, worship went longer than usual. I was engaged in worshiping the Lord, and all of the sudden a lady turned around and said, "Shonna do you have a song?" It startled me because I was not expecting someone to ask me if I had a song. Right then, a sense of fear rose up in me. I thought, Lord what are you doing? I quickly answered, "No, I don't have a song."

What I need to clarify at this point is that I'm not a singer. I would sing as a child, but had not done so in years, and surely not in church. After I gave her my answer, I thought, Glad I got out of that one.

In less than a minute, she turned back around, and this time she did not ask me, she told me with more authority in her voice and said, "Shonna, you have a song." At that moment, I knew it was the Spirit of God speaking to me. I heard His voice say, "I'm trying to do something. Now step out in faith and flow with me."

In fear and trembling, I told the lady that I had a song, and I began to walk toward the pulpit. I was arguing with the Lord saying, "You got me into this Lord, now get me out of it and give me a song because I don't have a song." Minutes turned to hours as I walked toward the pastor to take the microphone. The pastor asked me what I was going to sing. I still had no idea until he placed the microphone in my hand, then the song came on immediately. Relieved, I began to sing the song and flowed with the Spirit of God. I was amazed how God used my voice that night. I can say, it was all Him, I just yielded to His leading and gave Him my voice. God is faithful if we will step out in faith and flow with him.

As I traveled home the next day, the Spirit of God began to minister to me that I was to step into some new territory. He told me that in this next season I was going to help my pastors start a church and I was going to step out and lead worship. As I listened intently to Him, even though I had no idea how He was going to do it, I realized this was a great opportunity with divine timing. This was a life-changing invitation in which He began to interest me to do something I had not done before. A strong knowing rose up within me that I knew I was to say yes to this opportunity and trust Him to do the work in me and bring it out.

The hand of God was steadily guiding me into a new season with my pastors. It was quite apparent that He was about to stretch us and take us to a place we had not been before. He began enlarging me on the inside so He could show me some things to prepare for. He was stretching me for another gift to emerge, and boy was I nervous since I didn't have much training in this area. But I stepped into that season and allowed God to do a work in me for His glory. I didn't know I had it in me, but God knew, and He delighted in surprising me with another glimpse of who He made me to be.

GOD AS THE POWER SOURCE

In every season, if we allow God to lead us and we trust Him with another layer of our lives, we discover more of the treasures of our true identity. His word promises that we have everything we need to do what He has called us to do as well as get through whatever comes our way. Paul tells us in Phil. 4:13, "I can do all things through Christ to strengthen me." Many times, we don't know what we are capable of doing until a situation arises and requires it of us.

Times of adversity, or unexpected opportunities, often bring out another facet of our abilities. Which brings me to this question: Do you know what you are made of? Most of us have no idea what is deep down in us until we either face a crisis or we are presented with an exciting opportunity. We have no idea of what we are capable of doing or all that we can accomplish with God as our power source. It seems many times these situations bring out the very essence of our true identity and calling.

Most of us would rather stay in our comfort zone, but God has a way to push us out! It is those faith-stretching, water-walking moments—and even heart-wrenching moments—that seem to place a demand on the gifts inside us to come forth. These are hidden strengths within us that help us to become sharper and more resilient.

OPPORTUNITIES AND CHALLENGES REVEAL WHAT YOU'RE MADE OF

Have you ever had a day when you were going about your routine and suddenly, in a moment, everything changes? Maybe it was a patient coming into your office, or maybe it was a casual conversation at the airport while you are waiting for your flight? It might have been an unexpected phone call. We tend to see these moments as interruptions keeping us from going about what we need to do that day. But, in all actuality, these are divine interruptions from God giving us opportunities to answer His call and follow His leading.

God will often surprise us with opportunities to show us we have it in us do what He is calling us to do. We may think our life is insignificant - that we're not good enough, or that we are not equipped for the position, or even that we've missed our moment. However, it is never too late to come into God's plan for your life and let Him do a new thing in you.

The story of Rahab reminds us that we are significant and that there is a rich treasure on the inside of us. Rahab was known as a harlot, but she was much more than that. She was a strong business woman who made a living by running a tavern with her family. She had quite a reputation, but deep in her heart, Rahab longed for more. She longed for a life of purpose and meaning. She longed for a life of true love and fulfillment, not only for herself but also for her family. (Read Rahab's story in Joshua 2 and 6.)

Rahab is a great example of someone who was not aware of her potential on the inside. But, when faced with a divine interruption, then presented with an opportunity, she arose to save the lives of her family and herself. Rahab took a risk and trusted the Lord.

A suddenly-moment came to her one evening when two spies came knocking on her door and everything changed for Rahab. Something inside her knew this was an unusual moment. An opportunity came knocking that would bring change to her life and move her from a season of shame and captivity into a season of significance and purpose. God will always present an opportunity for deliverance and restoration to come to your house. It's up to you to open the door.

Rahab made a life-changing decision that night by opening her home to the spies and helping them escape, which in turn opened her heart to their God—and God revolutionized her life.

Somehow, she saw God's plan and purpose for her life. She began to understand that this divine interruption in her life was not just about her, but this was about what was in her, and what God wanted to do through her! This was about generations to come – this was about her legacy! For inside Rahab was the lineage of Jesus!

The power of redemption in Rahab's life brought her to a place of beauty and significance, known as a courageous woman. She left a legacy of faith in God instead of the legacy of shame. (She's mentioned in the faith chapter in the New Testament: Heb. 11:31.)

I'm sure Rahab had many disappointments throughout her life., but this night God had a divine appointment for her. She saw the opportunity and did not allow it to pass her by. She took it! Just as God had a divine appointment for Rahab, He has a divine appointment for you, too. No matter what decisions and choices you have made in the past that left you disappointed, God has a divine appointment waiting for you! Just as God preserved Rahab for purpose, He has preserved you too.

There is greatness inside of you that He has preserved to bring out. When times of doubt come, know that God always chooses you with purpose in mind. You have come through all the unsettling, crazy, shaky seasons of your life for His purpose. Rahab's disappointments and detours eventually led her into her destiny and into a life of fulfillment.

God is always up to something good in your life. He has divine appointments waiting for you in the future. You never know when a divine interruption will come with an extraordinary invitation to discover more of the treasures God has placed inside of you.

I believe God has brought you to a place that will require you to step into a new area of discovery in the destiny He has for you. There are some plans, ideas, and dreams that you've been holding in your heart for quite some time. Some of these may look small and seem insignificant, but God has purpose and significance in those things. He is purposeful in all He does in your life, and those ideas have purpose and maybe even attached to them. Because they do, it's time to move into them.

The Bible says He places His treasure in earthen vessels. He made an investment and deposited gifts and callings within us. He is our Creator and knows what is in us. As we thirst for Him, "as a deer pants for the water brook" (Ps. 42:1), He will unveil it as we make an exchange with Him in our intimate communion with Him. It's in the deep place of worship that He illuminates and conveys into our spirits His will and purpose for our lives.

Even if you don't know your own self-worth, you are a jewel—a great treasure, you are significant!

It's in YOU!

CHAPTER FIVE

WHAT IS YOUR FREQUENCY?

D o you have a favorite season of the year? A time when you are excited about life and looking forward to what that season brings. I love the autumn season leading into the New Year. I love everything about it— the weather, the food, the style of clothing and boots. I love watching the leaves change colors and feeling the crisp cool air as I go for long walks. There is always an excitement in the air, and people seem to be happier and more joyful.

Beyond all of that, I particularly love the autumn season because it brings a shift inside of me. My attention and focus become stronger for others, reaching out to them with the love of God. I also begin to draw near to God, tuning my ear into what He is saying for this hour.

Regardless of the time of the year, I believe our hearts always desire to start a new fresh season in our life. Something about starting the new year with a fresh start—setting goals, losing weight, getting a workout plan; but most importantly hearing the voice of God and getting His direction for the coming new year.

I can look back over my life and think of several times I have clearly heard God speak to me. Each time, my life was radically altered, moving me into a greater season of my destiny.

There's something about putting ourselves in remembrance of what the Lord has done for us in the previous year. How He brought supply and provision right when we needed it. Reflecting on how He brought us through the challenges and storms and showed us His faithfulness and goodness.

Being reminded of how He stretched us to reach for more that He wanted us to attain, and how He helped us to achieve it.

I'm inspired that God is always up to something in our lives and He always wants to stretch us in His plan. Whether last year was glorious or treacherous, this I know, God's BEST is yet to come. However, to continue the course, and come into the new things He has for us, we must hear His voice.

The most popular talent show on TV is The Voice. I enjoy watching the show as it inspires me to not only sing but to reach for more of the passions and desires God has placed within me. While watching The Voice one evening, the two words, The Voice, kept going over and over in my head and heart.

I thought of how many people want to hear God's Voice.

Then, the Spirit of God spoke to me and said, "My sheep hear My voice if they will tune their frequency to Me."

Jesus talks about hearing His voice in this passage:

"To him, the porter openeth; and the sheep hear his voice, and he calleth his own sheep by name, and leadeth them out. And when he putteth forth his own sheep, he goeth before them, and the sheep follow him: for they know his voice. And a stranger will they not follow, but will flee from him: for they know not the voice of strangers."

JOHN 10:3-5 (KJV)

Jesus strongly emphasizes that His sheep hear His voice. He did not say they can or they should. He simply said, "the sheep hear his voice," implying that they DO.

TV and radio stations fill the airwaves continually, all day every day, but we never hear them until we turn on the receiver and tune into the station. In the same way, we must put up our spiritual antennas, tune our frequency into God and His Word, and tune out the noises and voices in the world. Busyness is a time-stealer and distraction in our lives. We must get still before the Lord. Psalm 46:10 says, "Be still, and know that I am God."

HEARING GOD'S SOUND

God has a sound in the earth. That sound is what we call His voice. Jesus went to Bethany to awaken his friend Lazarus. You could say he went there for an awakening. When we say some-one awakens us, it's some voice that awakens us. There are many different kinds of voices. There is the voice of your alarm clock. There is a voice for your spouse - your kids. Then, there is the voice of traffic and horns. There is even the voice of our own bodies. So, we are generally awakened by sound. But, Jesus awakened Lazarus with His voice. That same voice that awakened Lazarus can awaken us. It is the voice of the Lord.

The voice of God or the sound of God is one of the most amazing things that we desperately need. In John 11:43 says, "When he had said these things, (speaking of Jesus), He cried out with a loud voice, Lazarus come forth." Lazarus was not just asleep; he was in a tomb, so Jesus was summoning him to come out of there. Jesus called him out, and even in the slumber of death, Lazarus heard the voice!

Isn't it amazing that God's voice is so awesome that when He speaks, living men will lay down and die, and dead men will rise up and live? God's voice has a distinctive sound. My question to you is: Do you recognize God's sound when you hear it?

Gen. 3:8 says, "And they heard the sound of the Lord God walking in the garden in the cool of the day: and Adam and his wife hid from the presence of the Lord God among the trees of the garden." Notice, when they heard God, they heard him walking. There was a sound that they heard when God was walking, not when God was talking. God has a sound that He can be identified from.

Did you know that you can understand the character of a person? When you hear something about them, perhaps you might say, "That doesn't sound like that person." When you know a person's character, you know the kind of things that they would say and would not say. So, you recognize their sound. For example, there are people in your life that have a bigger than life personality. When you hear someone say something like that person would say, you turn around and say, "That sounds just like so and so." You know that it sounds just like them because it reminds you of their character.

God also has a sound, and we have to learn how to recognize the sound so we can respond to that sound. Lazarus heard the sound of Jesus' voice, and he responded to it. He didn't just lay there. He heard His sound, and he responded in obedience. So, to hear means to obey.

It says in 2 Chron. 7:14, "If my people, which are called by my name, shall humble themselves, and pray, and seek my face and turn from their wicked ways; then will I hear from heaven, and will forgive their sin, and will heal their land." I want to point out in this scripture that God says, He will hear from heaven – meaning, he will answer and respond from heaven. God isn't saying He will just listen to you. He is saying that He will respond. Listening is passive, but hearing is active. When the Bible says, "Hear the Word of the Lord," it is saying obey it. It means, whenever you hear God, it demands a response. When you hear God's thunder, it shakes something in you. Not only hearing, but you feel Him because we hear through the vibration of sound waves. God sends out these waves, and we feel Him talking to us. The proof that we have heard Him is that we obey Him.

Are you listening for the sound of God in the cool of the day? This expression "cool of the day" actually comes from the Hebrew word Ruach, which means wind. When Adam and Eve were walking in the cool of the day, they actually heard the wind of God. The theologians say it should be translated as the wind of the storm. So if we say it like this, "they heard the wind of the storm walking in the cool of the day, and they went and hid themselves because they were afraid." We see here that they knew they messed up, and now they hear the wind of the storm. They were afraid and knew that God was coming in anger and judgment. They recognized His sound.

I'm sure whenever you were a kid, you could always tell by the sound of your mom's voice if she was hot, or when your dad had lost his mind. You knew when you heard that sound you better run and hide. Hearing that sound immediately produced a response in you.

God is speaking, but many are failing to recognize His sound. God's voice brings many things. His voice brings conviction, which inspires us to get right with God and align our life with Him. His voice brings comfort when you are upset. God's voice speaking to you says, "Be not afraid, for I am with you." Sometimes He will say to you, "Everything is going to be alright – I've got this, trust Me." Other times, He will bring conformation. He will speak a word through a person, and you realize this is conformation. Sometimes the Lord will deal with you in your spirit for you to go on a fast. Then, someone will bring up fasting, and you realize that this is not a coincidence, but it is a conformation. The voice of the Lord will confirm what He is saying to you. He will also confirm the Word to you.

God's voice brings clarity. Sometimes He may have told you something general about a situation; then God will bring clarity to the matter. He will bring a greater understanding of something He has spoken to you previously. Greater depth – greater clarity. God's voice also brings direction. He will say, "This is the way, walk in it."

I want to encourage you to practice hearing the voice of God. You have to practice being able to hear His sound. One of the best times to practice hearing God's sound is right when you wake up. Talk to God just like you would talk to your friend. Let Him know you love and adore Him. As you get in your car, talk to God. As you're at work, talk to God. Learn to practice the presence of God as you go throughout your day and you will begin to hear His voice (His sound) clearer.

Practice hearing God's sound through second thoughts. This is when you are about to do something and all of the sudden you have a second thought. There is a quickening in your spirit, which causes you to have a second thought. It's a check in your spirit – a red flag – a caution. This becomes that voice that says, "Something told me." Pay attention to second thoughts, because most likely the Spirit of God is getting your attention with this second thought to stop you from proceeding forward as a protection for you. It could be that this is not the opportunity for you to take, or perhaps you are not supposed to move into that house. Possibly you're not supposed to go anywhere with a certain person.

Many times, on paper, it may look like this is a reasonable choice, but all the sudden you have a second thought. The second thought says, "Don't do this." I was invited on a ministry trip and all the sudden my spirit was quickened, and I had a second thought, "Don't go." There had been a winter ice storm come though, and the streets and highways were in poor condition to travel on. I learned later there had been a severe accident with multiple cars on the highway about the same time I would have been traveling though. If I would not have followed the leading the Spirit with that second thought I had, I could have possibly been involved in the accident. In that situation, I did not hear an audible voice, nor did I get a scripture – I had a check in my spirit with a second thought, and I obeyed it. This is called responding to God's voice – It is responding to the leading of His Spirit. It will save your life!

Another way to practice hearing God's sound is to read the Bible in depth. Do not see how far you can read, but read it in depth and see what the Holy Spirit will show you. See how many verses you can get with understanding. Don't go far – go deep. Isaiah 28:10 says it is, "For precept upon precept, precept upon precept; line upon line, line upon line; here a little, and there a little." That's about depth. Ask the Holy Spirit to help you unpack the Word as you read it. You will be surprised that the strength of God will come just in one verse that becomes depth to you. It's those times when you are sick, and God gives you a verse that brings healing to you. Perhaps you are in trouble, and

God gives you a verse that becomes alive to you, and He says, "Fear not, for I am with you, don't anxiously look about you, for I am Your God. I will strengthen you, help you and uphold you." Perhaps, you don't know what to do, and He gives you a verse – all of the sudden, there is a strength that comes to keep you sound and stable. It is the depth of the Word that will keep you and stabilize you in very difficult circumstances.

Jesus will take you into the depths of the Spirit. He wants to take you into the deep waters. He is saying, "Get away from the edge and launch out into the deep." It is in the deep waters that you will catch the multitude of what God wants to give you. You have to get quiet and hear Him to launch out and receive what He has for your life.

It is in stillness, not the busyness that we tune our spiritual ears to hear the voice of God. The Lord always speaks to us in that still, small voice. "And after the earthquake a fire; but the Lord was not in the fire: and after the fire a still small voice." (1 Kings 19:12) When we get still before the Lord, we will not only hear His voice, but we will discover new qualities inside ourselves that He is calling us to use. Particularly the courage to be our authentic selves in all we endeavor to do.

Hearing God's voice is key as you walk out your destiny. God wants to awaken you to your divine God given purpose on the earth. He's looking for someone to talk to so He can give you the revelation of His plan. He says, "I know the plans I have for you; plans to prosper you and not to harm you, plans to give you a hope and a future." (Jer. 29:11) God knows the plan, but

He is looking for someone to talk to about them. He is looking for someone who has an ear to hear. He says, "My sheep hear my voice, and I know them, and they follow me." (John 10:27)

God's voice is the most precious thing we could ever get. I would be lost without it. It is my guiding light, daily.

WALK IN OBEDIENCE

When God calls us to do something with what He has put inside of us, we must act and walk in obedience, even when we don't see what He sees. If God says that we are warriors (or doctors, attorneys, teachers, artists, legislators, ministers, or whatever), then we can trust that this is true despite our insecurities and past experiences. He will change our perception of ourselves.

Gideon needed to hear the voice of God not only for direction but for encouragement. He needed to be built up and reinforced about the man God made him to be. He didn't see himself as God saw him.

Gideon saw himself as a coward in a time when Israel was facing great challenges. When times are hard, it is difficult to see the goodness of the Lord. We want to trust Him, but our circumstances seem hopeless, and many times, we lose faith. Not only do we lose faith, but sometimes our frequency has become fuzzy with surrounding noise around us.

Gideon was going about his work, and suddenly the angel of the Lord stood beside him, saying, "The Lord is with you, O valiant warrior!" Yet Gideon protests by saying that his family is the least in Manasseh and that he is the youngest, probably the weakest, and least-chosen in his father's house. (Gideon's story is found in the book of Judges.) Gideon responded to the angel in doubt and unbelief, thinking I don't look at myself as a valiant warrior and I doubt anyone else would ever consider me like that. (Or a doctor, a professor, a minister, an attorney, an entrepreneur, or any other profession God calls us to!)

DEFINING SELF

How do you define yourself? How do you introduce yourself? What identifiers do you use to describe yourself? Depending on what group of people you are with, most often that determines how you identify and define yourself. Through the years, most of us identify ourselves with the different roles that we have played in life. So much so, that we don't even think about how we introduce ourselves. It just comes out, and our identities and abilities turn into a label.

According to Gideon, he came from the least influential and least powerful tribe of Israel. He was the youngest and weakest in his family and was the least likely to do much. He didn't see in himself that he was more than someone who was hiding out while threshing wheat.

Sometimes we see ourselves this way. We don't see ourselves becoming more than where we are. We don't see ourselves starting a business. We don't see ourselves in a public setting praying, singing, or speaking when we have been asked. We limit ourselves because we don't think we have it in us. We are afraid of who we might become if we tried to stretch and enlarge ourselves.

LOOKING FOR A SIGN

God will be persistent in our lives. He will continually stir something on the inside of you until you come into agreement with His plan. We will continue to ask God, "Are you sure you want me to do that Lord?" Many will ask, "Can you show me a sign?"

Gideon set out a fleece and asked for a sign. The Spirit of God at that time did not live inside of people, so God would show them an outward sign to confirm His leading in their lives.

Today, we do not need to set out a fleece for a sign, because, as believers, we have the Spirit of God living inside of us. Therefore, God will speak to our spirit inside of us to lead us and confirm what He is saying to us. There will be a knowing so strong inside of us that we will know that we know—we will know it as well as we know our name. There will be no hesitation, for it will seem good to us and we will have perfect peace about it. Many times, God will bring other means of confirmation to us, but we are to always listen on the inside, and look for that perfect peace within.

One summer, I had gone to India to minister for six weeks. In other countries, you have to be very careful what you eat and drink. Several ministers and I had gone to a coffee/ice cream shop to get coffee and dessert. I ordered a small cold coffee with a scoop of ice cream. When I took a little sip of the coffee, something didn't settle right in me. It didn't taste quite right. It was so subtle that I could not put my finger on what it was. My flesh wanted that coffee, so I began to reason with myself, "I had this same drink just last week, and it was fine. I'm sure this one is okay."

What I didn't realize at the moment was, the Spirit of God was checking me in my spirit, trying to get my attention to let me know: "DO NOT DRINK IT – IT IS BAD." But, because my flesh wanted it, I reasoned about it, and my mind overruled the check in my spirit. I drank the coffee, and it nearly cost me my life.

I had to spend three days in the hospital in India before I could fly back to the States. It was a hard lesson to learn how to be led by the Spirit of God. I purposed in my heart that I would never reason anything out again, but that I would be sensitive—listening for the promptings and checks of the Spirit.

Gideon prepared a sacrifice and took it to God under the oak tree. This was a sacred place where he could tune into hearing God's voice. God met him there and showed him that the message from the angel was real.

HEAR THE VOICE BEHIND THE VOICE

Another frequency we need to tune into is listening for "The Voice" behind the voice. We hear His voice in our personal time praying and reading the Word, but we also hear His voice through preaching. It is "The Voice" behind the voice in a sermon that gives specific instructions. It is the Rhema Word behind the Word of God we read that brings revelations and life to our situation.

Psalm 29:4 says, "The voice of the Lord is powerful." He is saying the

power is in the voice. To have faith to do something, we must hear God's voice. Rom. 10:17 says, "Faith comes by hearing and hearing the word of God." Faith comes by hearing what we read in the Bible, but that's not all. What I read is going to be a beginning point to position me to hear God's voice. Because faith comes on the wings of a voice that I hear, I begin to read the Word of God; the implication is God will speak.

We have to hear what God has to say to us because what He says to us individually is what brings us success. It's a different - personal instruction than what He gives to another person. If we don't connect with the voice behind the sermon, we have no empowerment for faith to come into our life to do what He's calling us to do. When we take the Word of God, meditate on it and spend time with it; that's when we hear a voice behind that Word. That is when we get a Rhema Word from God that leads us into what God is moving us into. It's that Voice that becomes a voice of faith in our life, empowering us to go forth in what God tells us to do.

Gideon heard God's voice, but to reassure him, God confirmed it. He made it crystal clear that Gideon was indeed God's chosen leader, a valiant warrior who would save his nation. God knew it was in him, but Gideon would have never discovered it unless God called it out of him.

God is calling it out of you. He's calling forth boldness and courage to eradicate your fears and insecurities. He's removing the labels that others have placed on you, and He's showing you who you really are. When we know who we are, and who we belong to, we will always overcome any battle and come through victoriously. For God is with us!

It is time for you to see yourself the way God sees you. You have heard God's voice; now it is time for you to move forward in that. You have God's authority, anointing, power, strength, boldness, and courage.

It's in You!

CHAPTER SIX

RENEW THE MIND

One of the greatest hindrances to faith is thinking like the world thinks. The Bible says, "Be not conformed to this world: but be ye transformed by the renewing of your mind, that ye may prove what is that good, and acceptable, and perfect, will of God" (Romans 12:2, KJV). (Emphasis on the mind.)

God's thoughts from the Bible are supernatural thoughts. It is easy to block out those supernatural thoughts with natural thoughts that conform to the world's beliefs and standards. The pressure from the natural world is so great that most people accept bad reports, conform to them, and many times die because of it. We must not go by such natural deathly reports, but we should align ourselves with what the Word of God says; we should make it the final authority in our lives. We should believe what He says is true:

"(He) heals all your diseases" (PSALM 103:3).

"We have the mind of Christ" (1 CORINTHIANS 2:16).

Think His thoughts, not the world's thoughts. Act on His thoughts, not the world's thoughts. Then you will get His results, not the world's results!

The mind is the focal point of Satan's attack. He works at tormenting our minds to keep us in fear and despair—to keep us from achieving all that God has for us. Don't lend your mind to fear or condemnation and allow yourself to surrender to despair, but rule the kingdom of your mind by harnessing your thoughts. Instead, take every thought captive in the obedience of Jesus Christ (2 Cor. 10:5). If we change our mindset, we will change our future.

HOW WE DEFINE OUR LIVES

We define our lives by every thought and word that is spoken. If we want change to come about in our lives, we must control our thoughts and watch what we say, because it all starts there. "For as a man thinks in his heart so is he" (Prov. 23:7).

Our minds can get entangled with the world's way of thinking. Power lies within the Word of God to enable us to realign thoughts that have been misaligned by the world. This includes faulty mindsets, belief systems, traditions, and doctrines.

The devil's mode of operation is to get our attention through our thoughts. If the devil gets our attention, he has our life. He tries to get to us through circumstances. He wants us to focus on our problems. That will only take us on a downward spiral going nowhere and into a pit of despair. We must attend to God's Word, and incline our ear unto His sayings, for they are life and health to us. (Proverbs 4:20-22).

Every battle is won or lost in the mind arena. The Israelites refused to take possession of the land that God had prepared for them. They disobeyed God because they saw themselves weak and small. The enemy had convinced them they were as grasshoppers standing before giants. Because they bought into that lie, they were unable to fulfill God's call on their life. The enemy had paralyzed and bound them in fear, and because of that, the Giants were empowered.

What giants in your world are being empowered because of your fears? What are you allowing to paralyze you? What is stopping you from moving into what you know God is leading you to? It was fear alone that caused the Israelites to miss out on the promise of God. Don't miss out on God's promises for you. Don't let the enemy paralyze you and stop you from stepping into your next season. What you don't confront, you will never conquer. Confront your fears and be empowered by God's Word. Be bold and enter another season of your destiny.

SATAN COMES WITH WICKED WORDS

Satan comes with wicked words. Those wicked words are fiery darts that are targeted right toward us. This is a personal assault of Satan against believers. We wrestle against principalities and powers of the darkness; spiritual hosts of wickedness in high places. It's important that we put on the armor of God to quench every fiery dart of unscriptural words and thoughts.

Not only does the enemy come with thoughts in our own minds, he uses people to speak words to plant thoughts. Sometimes we think our fight is with people and their fight is with us. However, the Word says, we don't wrestle with flesh and blood.

Behind that person with whom you are having a disagreement, is a spirit influencing them. That spirit will speak lies, which is the enemy's tactics to cause discord in hopes to destroy. Perhaps that person is being influenced by listening to the wrong voices. By putting on the armor of God, we cover ourselves with the shield of faith to quench those fiery darts. Not only do we repel the assault of Satan against us, but we quench the thoughts that are targeted for our mind. When you find yourself in a situation like that, take your authority over those spirits and command the light of God to shine on the situation to bring truth and clarity.

The devil will do whatever it takes to keep you from moving forward and stepping out into your destiny. He will even come up with a plan to take you out of the game. However, when the devil has a plan to take you out, God has a plan to keep you in! I declare that word over you today—God has a plan to keep you in and moving forward.

TAKE THOUGHTS CAPTIVE

As I said earlier, fear can paralyze you from moving forward. I know in my own life, I have learned how to combat that fear with faith. I have learned to press through and do it afraid. I have learned to step into a place of total trust in God, knowing that He will see me through.

The Spirit of God ministered to me one time saying, "Fear is entering your mind through an uncontrolled imagination and thought life, and you are buying into the lie of the enemy. Take your authority and take those thoughts captive." The Bible says to take no thought (Matt. 6:25). We can't keep thoughts from coming, but we can keep from taking them in our life.

Have you ever gone through a difficult season in your life when thoughts were bombarding you and fear seemed to be taking you over? I have, and it was a very challenging time. The enemy was tearing me down because it seemed I had made a wrong decision in my life that would affect many other areas in the days to come. Thoughts consumed me – I couldn't seem to shake them. The enemy was doing everything he could to break me down emotionally to get me to quit, telling me every negative thing about myself that you could think of. BUT, God! When you are at your weakest, the Spirit of God comes in such a powerful way to strengthen, encourage, and teach you what you need to do. He ministered to me about who I am in Christ. He said, "Shonna, I want you to know who you are in Me. I want you to know it as well as you know your name is Shonna. I want you to write it out and give voice to it every day, especially when the enemy comes with lying vanity thoughts at you. Replace those thoughts with the truth of who you are in Me". As I began to do that many times throughout the day, fear, anxiety, and depression left me. Victory was mine!

Fear will gain entrance into our minds through an uncontrolled imagination and thought life. We have a choice. We can focus on the problem or even symptoms in our body, or we can choose to believe what God's Word says about us and meditate on His truths. Whichever one touches you, and becomes stronger in you, is the one that will possess you. What is touching your thought life is what will possess you. What is touching your mouth is what will take possession of you. Take authority and control over your thoughts. It is a God-given right to take those thoughts captive and command the devil to flee. Watch your thoughts and give fear no place in your life. Your thoughts are creating your life through the words you speak.

LEARN TO SIFT YOUR THOUGHT LIFE

We must learn to sift our thought life by filtering out anything we do not want to show up in our future. Instead, focus on what you truly desire. God wired our thoughts to have power so we would be equipped to overcome every obstacle. He fashioned us to create, innovate, strategize, and succeed. Just to be sure, He put his Divine thoughts and nature within us. Jer. 31:33 says: "I will put my instructions deep within you, and I will write them on their hearts." (NLT) Our heart and thoughts are connected, for our heart is controlled by our thought life. The heart becomes sensitive to what we choose to focus on. We must hook up our heart with the ultimate power source!

We must learn to identify the areas in our life where there is doubt, unbelief, and fear. These come to steal the blessing in our life. Ask the Lord to show you the truth in your inward man. Ask Him to show you where the root of that fear is so you can address it.

FEAR REALLY ISN'T IN YOU; IT'S WORKING THROUGH YOU.

"But they were terrified and frightened and supposed they had seen a spirit. And he said to them, why are you troubled and why do doubts arise in your heart?"

LUKE 24:37, 38 (NKJV)

Why do you entertain doubt and let doubt come? When we do not deal with the areas of fear in our soul, fear opens the door, and then we misread the Spirit. Fear causes us to lose discernment; when we lose discernment, we become troubled; when we become troubled, we doubt. That is the pattern, and it will cycle over and over in our lives until we take authority over that fear.

The key is to have a sound mind about the boundaries that God allows based on His word. Doubt and unbelief come from a lack of knowledge. When the Word says, my people perish for the lack of knowledge (Hosea 4:6), they are not perishing because they don't have any knowledge at all.

They are perishing because they don't have revelation on the matter and so they make choices that are "fear based." That causes trouble, and then they doubt. The enemy wants your thought life to be full of doubt, unbelief, and fear so you will give up on the dream and destiny that is inside of you.

HINDRANCES

Hindrances are a part of moving forward in the plan of God. Not hindrances from God, but hindrances from the enemy. Satan tries to bring hindrances to keep us from moving. Learn to not receive the hindrances, but to deal with them. Satan is after the movement of God. He is after the movement of people pursuing and actively engaging in the plan of God. He works tirelessly to hinder you. Firmly resist him.

Satan is defeated, but he is still active. Do not be ignorant of the enemy's devices and schemes (2 Cor. 2:11). He uses the words of other people and the power of suggestion to hinder progress in your life spiritually, mentally, and physically. He comes to hinder God's plan for our life. But, the Word says in Luke 10:19, "Behold, I give unto you power to tread on serpents and scorpions and over all the power of the enemy, and nothing shall by any means hurt you." Notice it doesn't say you will not be opposed, it says nothing will hurt you. It says, he gives us the power to tread... That means we have to do something. We must take our authority and do some walking over some things!

Years ago, I was ministering with a team in India for six weeks. We came up against many hindrances and road blocks that were set up by the enemy, but we were determined to fulfill and complete the assignment.

One particular incident happened the day we traveled to the Ganges River. The Ganges is a sacred river to Hindus. It is a lifeline to millions of Indians who live along its course and depend on it for their daily needs. It has been ranked as the fifth most-polluted river in the world.

Sadly, the Hindu people believe the water in the Ganges River is Holy and that it will bring healing to their bodies and prosperity for their families. This is one of the ways they please their god. They are told they have to visit the Ganges River at least once in their lifetime, to swim in it and even drink the water.

These areas are very hard to visit because your spirit is so grieved with all the sickness and disease you see. Lepers and beggars are lined up all around the area. The demonic activity is very strong in this area because the enemy doesn't want to let his people go. He wants to keep them bound and believing a lie about this river.

We walked into an area where we had to go through a gate to get to a certain building. The other ministers were slightly ahead of me and had already walked through the gate. I was about to go through the gate when a little girl came up from behind me and blocked my way. She placed a basket with a lid on it right in front of my face and glared at me with piercing eyes. Before I knew it, she removed the lid and in the basket was a black cobra! It was right in my face!

By the grace of God, I did not scream. Holy Ghost rose up in me, and I took authority over that spirit that ruled her. In an authoritative voice, filled with power, I said, "Jesus!" Then I said, "Move!"

As soon as I spoke, the little girl replaced the lid on the basket and moved out of my way, staring at me the entire time. The enemy in her wanted to see if I was afraid of him. He was trying to separate me from the other ministers, but his tactic didn't work. It ended up being a minor delay, but it could have been a life or death hindrance had I not known my authority in Christ and enforced it! We have power and authority in the name of Jesus. Exercise your authority and do not allow anything to hinder you moving forward with God's plan.

Satan tries to build an inroad into our life because he is after the Word. An inroad is something you do that will give him a place to enter. He is after the Word to keep you stuck and to keep you from prospering. Guard your thoughts and don't compromise. If you compromise, you are allowing him to come in and steal the Word in your life. Always walk in integrity and take the high road, for it will pay great dividends in your life.

LET THE WORD DWELL IN YOU

Let the Word of Christ dwell in you richly (Col. 3:16). Fill your heart so richly with His Word, for when you do this, it will help keep your thoughts in check.

When we allow the Word of Christ to dwell in us, the Spirit of God will serve us with a Word that we can live on. It will happen right when the enemy is attacking our mind. We will receive it right when you need it. The more truth we give the Spirit of God, the more we give Him to work within our lives. In other words, the more Word we put inside of us, and give voice to that, the more the Holy Spirit has to work with to bring things to pass in our lives. It matters the measure of His Word that is flowing in you. When the Word dwells in you richly, it will not only be enough Word for you to be victorious, but it will also be a Word for others to help them walk victoriously.

Also, we need to learn to work the Word that we receive and pray it out. Many people don't work the Word in their lives; immediately, the enemy comes to steal it. When you work that Word and pray it out, the Spirit of God will show you things and give you further instructions.

The degree to which we renew your mind will be the degree we will prosper. The degree to which we renew our mind will be the degree we will walk in health. What is the renewing of the mind? It means taking on what the Word says, which is God's thoughts. If you have thoughts that contradict the thoughts of God, then set your thoughts aside and say, "I'm not going to think those thoughts anymore, I'm going to think God's thoughts about my situation."

RENEW YOUR MIND AND
CHANGE YOUR PERSPECTIVE

Perspective is a powerful thing. Perspective is a particular attitude toward or way of regarding something; a point of view. To come into the destiny God has for us, you must see His perspective concerning everything in our lives. We must renew our mind to His thoughts and His ways, and it will change our perspective to see what is right and true.

Whatever lens we're looking through, will determine what we think and perceive. What lens are you looking through? Looking through the lens of the world brings fear, anxiety, depression, and discontentment. But, looking through the lens of the Word brings life, peace, joy, and abundance.

One word from God will change a person's whole perspective and perception. One word from God will shift wrong thinking and bring forth His thoughts and wisdom for a situation you are facing. One word from God will cause sight to return where the enemy has had blinders on you. When we renew our minds to God's perspective, it will cause fresh vision to spring forth. Renewing your mind to His perspective is the key to advance and tap into the things God has put inside of you.

Have you felt like you have been carrying weight in some areas of your life—possibly dragging your feet due to circumstances around you? Maybe you're not able to clearly see the direction the Spirit of God wants to take you concerning some things. If you get into the Word and begin to renew your mind, God will change your perspective on how you currently see things. When your perspective changes, your position changes. When your position changes, you will experience promotion because God will propel you forward. The opportunities God has for you will begin to present themselves. Things you need will be assessable to you. People that God has ordained to be a help to you will willingly offer their services for the assignment He has given you.

Your perception has everything to do with your advancement and how this year will work for you. The enemy's job is to keep you focused only on the things you see in the natural, which alters your mindset of possibilities in God. Let God change your mind and perception. Guard your thoughts, for as a man thinks in his heart so is he (Prov. 23:7). See through the eyes of faith and move forward.

It's in YOU!

CHAPTER SEVEN

UNLOCK YOUR MASTERPIECE

What are you custom-made for? God has tailor-made you for something very specific. What passions burn within your heart? God is calling on your potential. He wants to unlock the masterpiece that dwells in you and bring out your greater potential. There are seeds that lie dormant in you that won't come alive until they are placed in the right soil to spring forth. Do you know where He has placed you? This will be where your potential will be unlocked, and provision will come forth.

Years ago I had an opportunity to travel to Italy. I have always wanted to go to Italy and experience the Italian culture —the beautiful scenery, delicious food, the music—in which Andrea Bocelli in one of my most favorites. Of course, I wanted to experience the exquisite art and most certainly their fashion and shopping as well. A trip to Italy would be incomplete for a girl who loves fashion! There are so many lovely things to see in Italy; a person could stay for months.

I was particularly excited to visit the art museums. One of the museums that we toured displayed Michelangelo's unfinished art. The museum had many pieces of incomplete statues that he never finished. They are referred to as incomplete magnificent illustrations. As I went through the room, I noticed some of the statues were almost finished but lacked certain pieces of the body to complete it. One had a missing head; several had hands missing and so on. There were others that didn't have much to them at all.

My friend commented to me, "Can you imagine what these finished pieces of art could have been?" I was just thinking that myself, but had not voiced it yet. Right after that, the Spirit of God ministered to me and said, "You can liken that to many of My children that have not come into their purpose (calling). They have a masterpiece within them that they know not of. Some have come into their calling, but have gotten off coarse and will not fulfill their purpose unless they return to their true love. Others have not come into it at all."

I was taken aback by what I perceived I heard. It captured my attention so intently that I immediately humbled myself and repented for not aligning myself completely to what I knew in my heart and where my attention needed to be focused. I sat down for a minute so I could write out what I heard. I wanted to make sure I wrote down every word as clear as I heard it. I planned on going back to it later to ask the Holy Spirit to minister more to me on that.

Advance two years forward and the Spirit of God began to minister to me again about that particular moment. I began to think of all the people that never fulfilled their purpose and finished their course the way God designed for them. My heart became concerned as I reflected on my own life. I immediately told the Lord I didn't want that to be me—I want to fulfill the purpose and plan He destined me for. I didn't want to come up short in any way, but I wanted Him to use me in every capacity that He desires. I told Him I wanted to discover everything that He has put in me for His purposed and His glory.

That day I had one of those defining moments with the Lord that shifted my priorities and perspective. I decided from that day on I would purpose to live out of my eternal purpose in Christ and be eternally minded. I desired Him to make me into the masterpiece He desired for me to be.

Michelangelo's sculptures and paintings rank among the most famous in existence. His work is displayed in the most elite museums around the world. But, the art he left unfinished remained in this museum in Italy. These unfinished pieces never reached their full potential. The artwork lacked significance and remained unnamed and unseen compared to his finished work.

Maybe you can identify with the unfinished pieces that never reached their full potential. You may feel insignificant, unfinished or undone. Maybe you're wondering if you will ever reach your full potential. Perhaps you are thinking of what you could have been, but that it is too late now.

Can I tell you, it is never too late to let God work His masterpiece in you. Whatever disappointments you have had in the past, God has a divine appointment for you. He has a divine appointment with you!

You may feel insignificant. You may wish you were completely different from the way you are. Perhaps you wish you were more intelligent, more gifted, more attractive—maybe even born into a different family. God knew what He was doing when He created you. God fashioned and formed you down to every fine detail just the way you are because He saw it was perfect and complete. You are who you are so that you can fulfill your destiny. You are God's masterpiece.

UNLOCKING YOUR HEART

There are promises in your heart that God wants to make alive again. What do you see yourself doing? Your feet will never take you where your mind has never gone. If you can perceive it, you can receive it and become it. God will shine His light on you, to bring forth revelation revealing your potential. We know the entrance of His Word brings light and revelation, so when we get light on a matter, faith will come alive in our hearts to perceive and see what is inside of us. He has already crowned us with favor, and favor determines the limits of our destiny.

Have you felt cramped up, stationary, or too fixed? God

wants to unlock your heart with new ideas, strategies, and instructions with what you are to do and where He is sending you. He wants to unlock the greater potential that is inside of you. Potential refers to the hidden abilities. You have hidden abilities in you that need to be discovered. There are gifts that the Lord has deposited in you. Your potential is unlimited with Him.

THERE IS MORE IN YOU

Don't be restricted by where you came from, for there are gifts and talents in you of which you are not even aware. Where God is taking you? These gifts will be needed, and they will come out! God wants us to have the attitude that there is more to us than what we see. So believe in yourself and ask the Holy Spirit to draw them out!

Listen to what Paul says about this:

"For we are His workmanship, created in Christ Jesus for good works, which God prepared beforehand that we should walk in them."   EPH. 2:10 (NKJV)

Here's the New Living translation of that verse:

"For we are God's masterpiece. He has created us anew in Christ Jesus, so we can do the good things he planned for us long ago."

More Scriptures to let you know that God is in control:

"Know that the Lord, He is God. It is He who has made us and not we ourselves."   Ps. 100:3 (NKJV)

"Your hands have made me and fashioned me. Give me understanding that I may learn your commandments."

Ps. 119:73 (NKJV)

You are God's masterpiece. You are exceptional and unique in your own design. He has formed and fashioned you. You can rest assured that God will finish, complete, and perfect that which concerns you. Paul tells us in Phil. 1:6, "...He who has begun a good work in you will complete it until the day of Jesus Christ." He will complete the masterpiece He ordained you to be.

When we know we are His masterpiece; it changes the way we walk into a room. It changes the way we look at ourselves. It changes the way we react to what people say about us. When we know we are His masterpiece; we rise above inferior feelings. Feelings are fickle, and they most certainly lie to us. Feelings tell us we are unworthy and undeserving of the goodness of God. Feelings tell us what we do is not good enough. Feelings keep us in bondage if we let them. We must learn to shake off those feelings and tell ourselves we are royalty because that is what we are. God wants you to see yourself as a king and a priest unto Him, because that is who He has made you to be.

THE MEASURE OF YOUR WORTH

At different times in our lives, we have felt shame over something that we have done. Perhaps we have even felt shame because of our thoughts. We might have felt unworthy based on our actions or even something terrible that has happened to us. Our worth is not based on who we are, but whose we are. It's not based on what we have or haven't done; it's based on what He has already done. It is the finished work of Jesus Christ in us. We are inherently valuable to God, and He has already made us His masterpiece. When this revelation comes alive inside, it changes the way a person thinks and speaks. It changes the way you carry yourself. It is at that moment you start to walk in who you really are.

Our worth is not based on how much money we make, what kind of house we live in, or what kind of car we drive. It is not based on how pretty we are, or how skinny we are. It is not based on what brand of clothes we wear or what handbag we carry. Our worth is not based on any of these things; these things are carnal. Life is not about the beauty on the outside, or what we could attain on our own. God looks at our beauty on the inside, and all the spiritual things He has deposited in us.

We discussed in the last chapter about how David was overlooked because his family had judged him on appearance. In 1 Samuel 16, God sent Samuel to Jesse's house to anoint the next king of Israel, telling Samuel that He had provided a king among Jesse's sons.

When Samuel arrived, He had Jesse call for his sons. When he looked at Eliab, he said, "Surely the Lord's anointed is before Him!" But the Lord said to Samuel, "Do not look at his appearance or at his physical stature, because I have refused him. For the Lord does not see as man sees; for man looks at the outward appearance, but the Lord looks at the heart" (1 Samuel 16:6, 7).

YOUR HEART

God looks at the heart, and He wants us to live from our heart. Life passes through the heart, so we are to guard our heart with all diligence. Out of it flows the springs of life and it determines the course of our life (Prov. 4:23). When the heart is pure, and the heart is clean, there is an unlimited possibility for where God can take you.

God doesn't just look at the heart; He looks into the heart. Based on what He sees, He decides whether to promote or not. The enemy works tirelessly to put boundaries in our heart that will detour and stop the flow of our destiny that God has planned for our life. Don't let negative things take up residence and live in your heart. Otherwise, it will taint your masterpiece. We must let go of all disappointments, envy, bitterness, unforgiveness, and even pressure. We must let it pass through our heart. Otherwise, the heart can become sick with disappointment and eventually the heart will harden. I have learned it is a hardened heart that dulls a person's ability to perceive and understand who they really are.

Jesus spoke to His disciples in Mark 8:17 about the characteristics of a hard heart. In these verses, He gives us symptoms that are descriptive of a hard heart: (1) unable to perceive, (2) unable to understand, (3) unable to see, (4) unable to hear, and (5) unable to remember. These describe inabilities in the spirit.

When our heart becomes hardened, it hinders our ability to see the masterpiece we are designed to be, and it stops the supernatural power of God from flowing in our lives. But, when we keep our heart tender and humble before the Lord, there will be a continual flow.

YOUR THOUGHTS

What thoughts do you think about yourself? Do you struggle with negative thoughts because of a dysfunctional past? One way Satan comes to steal your inheritance and destiny from you is by bombarding you with negative thoughts about yourself. His thoughts lead to destruction, but God's thoughts lead to inspiration and life. Satan tells you that you are less than others around you and that you don't matter.

These are tools in his arsenal he uses to steal your true identity and your masterpiece. Satan understands seed-time and harvest. He plants a seed in us, then gets us to repeat what he planted. He works at shifting our focus over to the negative things he has said about us. Next, he waits to see if we will nourish the seed he planted by thinking and meditating on those things. He is persistent in trying to get us to give voice to what he planted in us so that we will live and rehearse those thoughts all day long. He knows if we rehearse those thoughts and give voice to them, we will attract exactly what we are thinking and saying.

What you are attracting will tell you who you are inside.

Many people need to decide to stop acting and thinking like they're acting and thinking, so they'll stop attracting what they are attracting. Eventually, you will reap a harvest of your negative thought life if you don't change it.

REJECTION

Many times, I have seen rejection from people's pasts hinder them and hold them back from their full potential in Christ. When we have been rejected in the past, it has the potential to open up a wound. It is hard to heal the wound of rejection. If we are not careful, we end up carrying that with us throughout our life.

Whether you have been rejected by family, friends, coworkers, leadership, or church, be aware—it greatly affects your life. When that rejection comes from somebody you care about and trust, it can cause intense pain. That pain affects everything in our life all the way through, from childhood to adulthood. It can affect your job, your marriage, your relationships, your view of God, and how you worship. God wants to heal you of the pain that is associated with rejection. God wants you to understand that no matter who has rejected you, He has accepted you completely. You are accepted in the beloved (Eph. 1:6).

When you suffer rejection, you begin to look for acceptance in any number of different places and different ways. For instance, instead of working forty hours a week, you'll start working fifty hours a week, because you're trying to perform your way into acceptance.

COMPROMISING CONVICTIONS

Sometimes, to gain acceptance, we wind up compromising our convictions. Convictions are deep-rooted beliefs within us. When we are convicted of something, we must stay true to who we are at the core and our true identity. Unfortunately, many begin to compromise their convictions to be accepted.

When we start compromising our convictions to be accepted, it can influence the way we dress and how we speak; it can influence how we act and the places we go. Rejection can even affect our decision making. It will cause us to compromise decisions we make.

Perhaps you shared your career dreams with someone who then laughed at you. You are now unable to shake the fact that you were laughed at so you compromise your career path. What has happened? You've allowed someone's laughter (rejection), to stop you from fulfilling your dream. You have denied the passion inside of you by choosing another career path.

You do not have to run after acceptance in your life; you need to know you have a God who wants to give it to you as a gift. You are already accepted in the beloved. When you truly get that revelation, you will walk with authority and will speak with authority. It will put a strong backbone in you and will crush that feeling of desperation. You are somebody. You are the child of the Most High. You have been accepted in the beloved, and you carry within you the Name that is above all names (Phil. 2:9).

You have been accepted by God's grace. It is His gift to you. Grace is God's loving-kindness. It is His undeserved and un-merited favor towards us. Grace is His acceptance of us, and His influence upon our heart that turns us to Christ. It is the fullness of His benefits and His bounty. Because God's grace has accepted you, you don't have to look for acceptance in any area of your life. All you need is His grace to become more like Him, which in turn allows Him to unlock your masterpiece within. God's acceptance and grace are all you need to fulfill your destiny call.

GOD KNOWS WHERE YOU ARE

Put on your royal apparel and become who God made you to be in Christ. The more you comprehend who you really are in Christ, the easier it becomes for you to manifest the truth about yourself. When you know your identity, no one can take your destiny. No one can push you out of your destiny. Even if your family overlooks you as David's family did, God knows right where you are. He will bring you in from the field and position you right where you need to be. When you honor God and believe God has chosen you, it will cause you to get better and not bitter.

Even though you may have gone through some hurtful situations, God will use those hurts in your life to propel you forward. I can't imagine the pain and rejection Joseph must have felt when he was sold into slavery. Then he was thrown into prison for choosing purity (Gen.39:20).

There are times you have to go through something to gain something. Joseph went to the pit to get to the palace. The Children of Israel went through the desert to get to the Promised Land. Paul went through the storm to get to Rome. But God was with them through it all and took them to a place of blessing.

Even in all the heartache that Joseph went through in his journey, the favor of God on his life propelled him into what God had custom-made him to become. He stepped into his true identity, purpose, and divine destiny.

Never lose faith and distance yourself from God, because God is on your side. He is working things out on your behalf. Never allow yourself to give up on God's ability to transform your life into something beyond your imagination. He knows what's inside of you better than you do.

When you don't see a way, He will make a way and reveal it to you. Mark 4:22-25 (AMP) says, "For nothing is hidden, except to be revealed; nor has anything been kept secret, but that it would come to light [that is, things are hidden only temporarily until the appropriate time comes for them to be known]." God will make it known to you in His perfect time. Even if you feel like you have come to an end and there is nothing left, God will reveal to you that he has put a tenacity inside of you.

God placed it inside of you just like He placed it inside of Joseph. You may feel like you have no power or strength, but God has put resilience in you that comes alive when you face adversity. There was resilience in Joseph that became the very essence of who he was. Hit after hit, Joseph continued to stay motivated and pressed on. It was the call of God on his life, as well as the grace/favor of God that sustained him and kept him on the course toward his destiny. What the enemy meant for his harm, God used it for his good to propel him toward his purpose.

The same is true for you. What the enemy plans to use to destroy and derail you from your destiny, God will turn it around and use it to propel you. Your employer may think he is firing you, but what's really happening is he is lighting a fire within you that will direct you to a better job with better benefits. Others may think they are robbing you, but they are only making room for the blessing of God to come in and overtake you.

In the midst of your largest losses, and most devastating rejections, remember that God is all-powerful and all-knowing. He will carry you through that grief and bring you back into the light with purpose and passion.

Joseph knew from a very young age that he was special, but he never knew all that he had inside of him until circumstances tried to crush his spirit and take him out. He didn't know that his confidence in the Lord would sustain him, carry him through, and eventually elevate him to a position of power to save millions of people. Joseph didn't know he had all of this inside of him, but God knew.

God knows what is inside you, too. Trust Him to continue to tailor-make you, preparing you for all He has ahead. Press on with confidence and know God is orchestrating even the most difficult situations in your life to be used as a catalyst for His kingdom. You are His masterpiece!

It's in YOU!

CHAPTER EIGHT

DESTINY ETCHED WITHIN

Recently I was visiting with a good friend of mine. We were talking about monumental moments in our lives. Moments that mark your life and change the course of your destiny. These are defining moments in life that mark you that are undeniable and irrefutable, and you are never the same again. You are awakened and forever changed. These moments are highly significant and hold a very special place in your heart. During our conversation, I thought, "In all the defining moments in life, one that would be in the top five for me, would be when I discovered my purpose in life—what God called me to do."

Many people don't discover why they were born and their purpose until later in life. I happened to ponder that question at an earlier age of 22 but came to a life-changing moment at the age of almost 25 when I became desperate to know what my purpose was in life. I wanted to know why God had me here on earth and thought surely there was more purpose in life than what I was already doing. Questions arose in my mind—Why was I born? What was I supposed to do with my life, what I was doing was not fulfilling? What would God's plan be for me if I surrendered to His plan?

While in college, I did not particularly ask these questions. I had my plan and my agenda. I thought I had it all figured out. I was in dental hygienist school, but I knew that was not my destiny. It was just a starting place to take me to the next adventure. Once I graduated college, I moved to Switzerland to take my first job; I wanted to travel the world. My idea was to travel Europe for a year, then return home. A fun and adventurous plan, yet I did not know what was ahead for me. Circumstances cut my experience of working overseas short, and I returned home.

After returning home, I was working full-time in the dental office but had a dream in my heart to run my own business and be a motivational speaker. Motivational speaking has always been a big dream of mine, as I love to motivate people to walk out their destiny and reach their full potential. It is a strong passion that I carry and it threads throughout everything I do. I was busy working on many things—an overachiever to say the least. The only problem was, these were MY ideas and MY agenda, not God's.

I do not recall any messages in church about destiny and

purpose when I was growing up—at least not like you hear to-day. Today, destiny and purpose is a hot topic—along with your identity in Christ and reigning with Him today. My parents always told me I could be whatever I wanted to be. They encouraged me and put me in everything from dance and singing to sports and cheerleading because I was so outgoing. They were my number one cheerleaders, that is certain. I am so grateful because it instilled in me that I CAN do anything I put my mind to do and I did.

I was raised in a Baptist church, so I knew the message of salvation. But, I was never taught about healing, deliverance or even much about faith regarding the Spirit of Faith. I knew I had the victory in Jesus because we would sing it every Sunday! However, I missed asking God about His plan and purpose for my life and the destiny He has called me to. I don't ever recall asking God what He desired for me because the enemy would whisper to me telling me if I surrendered my life to God, He would make me be a missionary, and I would be poor. It sounds so silly today because I love to travel to the nations for ministry purposes. But, at that time, I didn't have a true definition of a missionary. In my mind, I thought all they did was hand out food, and they were poor. I was certainly too ambitious to be poor, so I knew that was not for me.

I continued planning my own course and my own way, not fully realizing God's plan would be the best for me, and that mine would only lead me down a path of unfulfillment. But, after having an encounter with God and surrendering my life and everything about me to Him, I began attending a Charismatic church and one of the first versus I heard was Jeremiah 29:11, "For I know the plans that I have for you," declares the Lord, "plans for welfare and not for calamity to give you a future and a hope." I thought, it this is what God's Word says then surely His plan for my life will bring me fulfillment.

I would often visit my dad at his office, and while I was there, he would read the Word to me. I have never forgotten the verse he read in Prov. 19:21, "Many plans are in a man's mind, but it is the Lord's purpose for him that will stand (be carried out)." It was at that moment that it dawned on me God has ordered my steps in His plan and that it would be greater and much more rewarding than anything I could ever do on my own.

I remember when I was in Bible school Rom. 8:28 came alive to me in a new way. I had heard this verse many times, "All things work together for good to them that love God, to them who are called according to his purpose." But this time, I read it in a new light. I found out this promise is not for everyone, it is exclusively to those who "love God" and are "called according to his purpose."

For the first time, I realized how much I needed God's purpose more than anything else in my life. If I were walking out His purpose in my life, He would cause all things to work together for good for me, even if I missed God. I am grateful because there have been times I have missed God. Because He is so merciful, good and has a covenant with His word, His grace abounds to my account working any mistake I have ever made for my good. There will be times when we make a mess out of things and miss the mark. But when you and I are in His purpose, He has promised to work it all for good.

The older I have gotten, I have become more aware that life is short. James says, "Life is but a vapor" (James 4:14). I'm quite aware that the season I am in is but for a short time. Even those who I love dearly, will not be here with me forever. Therefore, I cherish every moment I have with them. The older we get, it seems that time does fly, and because it does, we must master and seize the moment!

None of us have time to waste, yet so many do it every day living only for themselves and their desires instead of choosing God's desires and plan. Many fail to discern the difference between what we want for us and what God has purposed for our destiny. Full of our own ideas, we set out with our plans asking God to bless them. We end up trying many different things only to find ourselves empty, unfulfilled and sometimes even broke.

As a young woman in my early 20s, I was very ambitious and highly motivated. Even though I had graduated from the University of Oklahoma, and received my degree and license to practice dental hygiene, it was not enough. I had an entrepreneur mindset and desired to own my own business. I had dreamed of opening a coffee shop/bookstore before Barnes and Noble ever existed. There was this new, hip coffee shop my friends and I went to often. The ambiance of the place was so inviting and relaxing—just a great place to hang out.

One afternoon, I was visiting with the two young guys that

owned the business. I talked them into giving me a part-time job (along with my full-time job) so that I could learn the business, in hopes of possibly opening a coffee shop/bookstore one day. In addition to practicing dental hygiene and the part-time job at the coffee shop, I was also building another business. But, above all those things, my strongest passion and heart's desire was to be a business motivational speaker. Therefore, I was working on that as well. Did you ever sleep, you ask? Very little it seems. I didn't have time to sleep if I was going to accomplish all of this.

At this point, I'm moving forward, building my life on the wrong foundation not realizing I was building it in vain. I had my desires, ambitions, plans, and strategy, and I was asking God to bless it all. One day, it all seemed to cave in on me, and I asked myself, "What am I really doing?" I was busy building my life the way I thought I wanted it and with what I thought would make me happy. However, I found myself miserable, depressed, heavy-hearted, desolate, perplexed and unfulfilled in every way.

Aren't you glad God never leaves you nor forsakes you? His eye is always on you waiting for you to call on Him for help. As soon as we do, He shows up with such peace, comfort and love to lavish us with. After finding myself miserable in a life that looked wonderful, prosperous and exciting to the world's eye, I came to the end of who Shonna was. I cried out to God and asked Him to show me His destiny for my life.

The Bible says, "Unless the Lord builds the house, they labor in vain who build it." We need to understand that our true fulfillment will be found in seeking first the Kingdom of God and what God has purposed for us. Our destiny is found in the Kingdom. God has a plan with a divine purpose for every person, and it is found in His kingdom. We need to let Him build our house—our life. The key to every success and every fulfillment in life is to seek first the Kingdom then ALL other things will be added unto you. (Matt. 6:33) "All other things" includes knowing your destiny.

God created you and me for the destiny He has for us, not for Him to help us with our plan for our life. Our "calling" is wrapped up in our obedience to His plan. He created us to thrive and successfully complete His plan, which is advancement of His Kingdom all for His glory. The Apostle Paul tells us, "For us, there is but one God, the Father, from whom are all things and we exist for Him; and one Lord, Jesus Christ, by whom are all things, and we exist through Him" (1 Cor. 8:6).

We exist in God's Kingdom, not our kingdom. Our destiny is to fall in love with the people our calling gives us access to. It is the people that we are called to that become our destiny, not our gift. Our destiny involves His plan for His glory, not our glory. Col. 1:16-17 says, "By Him, all things were created, both in the heavens and on the earth, visible and invisible, whether thrones or dominions or rulers or authorities—all things have been created through Him and for Him. He is before all things, and in Him, all things hold together".

Notice that it doesn't say, "All things have been created through Him for you." God created all things through Him and for Him. You have bee created for God Himself. Not only that, but it also says God is before all things; meaning—He is first in all things. Living out our destiny is all about proper alignment—God's order and way of doing things. God wants to be first in our lives, and when we put Him first, then all things will hold together.

If your life is falling apart, and you find yourself miserable and depressed, if you feel like you are losing it and your lacking peace and stability, the first thing you need to ask yourself is, "Am I putting God first in my life and am I asking Him for His plan for my life?" God must be positioned before all other things in your life in order for Him to hold those things together. It is only when you position Him first that you will find true peace, joy, and fulfillment allowing Him to build your house—your life—your destiny.

So many people lack peace and stability in their life. They suffer emotionally and many times physically because they don't seek first the Kingdom of God. They don't position Him before all things in their life. God will hold the plan of your life together only when He comes before everything else in your life.

The Apostle Paul shines more light on this in Eph. 1:9-11. "He made known to us the mystery of His will, according to His kind intention which He purposed in Him with a view to an administration suitable to the fullness of times, that it, the setting up of all things in Christ, things in the heavens and things on the earth. In Him also we have obtained an inheritance, having been predestined according to you His purpose who works all things after the council of His will."

God empowers us according to His purpose, not according to our wants and desires outside of His purpose. If you are living outside of God's plan for your life, you are missing out on the fullness of His power that He has for you. You're not experiencing God's highest and best with you to the maximum potential because you are building on your own foundation. What He has planned for your life is far great than you could ever dream of on your own or achieve yourself.

David was a man after God's own heart. He was not a perfect man, but he served the purpose of God. We see in Acts 13:36, "Now when David had served God's purpose in his own generation, he fell asleep; he was buried with his ancestors and his body decayed."

David did what he had been called to do on earth. He knew it wasn't all about him. David realized his destiny was tied to God's desire and that his purpose, his blessings that he received and all God has for him flowed out of his destiny.

If we truly want to discover and live out the fullness of our destiny, we have to put God first and seek His kingdom for our life. Like David, we have to realize it is not all about us and our desires, but it is about others and God's purposes through us.

It is a time like never before to know God's plan for our life and get busy in it. Carpe diem—seize the day—the moment! There are things you and I may want, but we need to be open and honest with God to the degree that we say to God, "As much as I want this or that, if it's not Your highest and best for my life, please show me, so I will let it go and re-direct my focus."

We must also understand that sometimes, just because we haven't received something yet that we feel God has said is ours, it does not mean it's not His plan. Whatever is in His will and plan He has permitted us to receive. That is why it imperative that we know His will and purpose. My question to you is: What has God given you to possess that you don't know about yet, simply because you don't know His purpose for your life?

Who has God said you are to become? Is there a leader inside you that you have not seen yet? Do you feel like there is more, deep down inside you than what you are currently seeing? Could it be that you have been comfortable in your comfort zone with your life set on cruise control, afraid to let God accelerate you because of insecurity, not feeling adequate or possibly lack of finances and other resources? Could it be that you have been so content in this season of your life that you are about to miss an effectual door of opportunity that God has divinely orchestrated and ordained for you?

I love the story of Esther. Esther was a young Jewish orphan girl living with her cousin Mordecai. Her family had been killed during the first Babylonian invasion, so Mordecai adopted Esther and was raising her as his own daughter. Mordecai and Esther were both captured during the second Babylonian invasion and were exiled to Persia. While they were living in Persia, Mordecai decided to change Esther's name Hadassah meaning "myrtle tree," to Esther, a Persian name meaning "star". Mordecai changed her name to disguise her ancestry to protect her. I think Esther's new name fit her well. Like a star, Esther's sparkle and brilliance allowed the light of God to shine through her in a dark time to a dark generation.

Esther was a woman who had destiny etched within her, yet she had no idea. She did not know what was inside her until the opportunity arose that God ordained her for.

Are you like an Esther? Is there a courageous woman inside of you despite that fact that you feel inadequate? If so, may I be the one to remind you that whenever God calls us to something, He has already equipped us and knows that we are fully capable of doing so. He would never ask us to do something without giving us what we need to do it successfully.

When He calls us, He qualifies and equips us for the task at hand. He would never send His children into a battle without training and equipping them. If He has called you by a new name, then let it tell you who you really are, whether you see it or not. The name denotes nature. Hadassah's name was changed to Esther. I believe the real reason God had Mordecai change her name to Esther was because the light of God in her would shine through her as she rose up in strength and courage in the battle she found herself in for her nation.

When you begin to notice, God is changing your nature and character; you need to acknowledge that and say, "Yes God, I receive that," then rise in courage and strength and seize the opportunity God has ordained you for.

Esther was a young woman who literally changed the world around her by standing alone for God. Her life may have seemed insignificant and ordinary to some, but in God's hands she did the extraordinary and became a woman of destiny. Only God knows how to prepare us for the next step in our life, especially when it seems beyond our own ability to imagine.

Often God inspires us to be strategic, innovative and resourceful to accomplish what He's told us to do. However, it's not by might, nor by power, but by His Spirit that ultimately wins our battles. When we rely on God, we know we can't lose because He's a God through whom all things are possible. When we rely on him, He calls us by name, so we know who we are and whose we are. When we know that, we will always overcome because that is who we are—overcomers!

People of destiny cannot "hide their lights under a bushel," rather, they must be bold! We must not be afraid, but courageous and give it our all for God is with us! Isn't it time you arise and release what God has put inside of you? You may not see it, feel it or even believe it, but you've got it! Release it and let it go!

It's in YOU!

Chapter Nine

Your Signature Voice

H ave you ever been drawn to someone? There was just something about them that caught your eye - your attention. Maybe it was the way they talked or how they carried themselves. Perhaps it was their generosity or their genuine desire in knowing and helping you. Whatever it was, they impacted your life, and it made a difference in you.

People are drawn to and influenced by leaders who communicate authentically and connect easily with people in a positive way. These people seem to have an immediate impact on a person. It has been my experience in this walk with the Lord and the calling He has given, that there will be a few people that leave a significant mark on your life. It is a mark that is undeniable and irrefutable. It is not only their anointing and charisma, but it is their genuine heart and love for people, which I believe makes up a big portion of their signature voice.

These leaders make a heart connection and invest in hearts - they literally impart to the heart. They are not just there to perform and deliver a good message, but they literally carry a love for people, and they impart into the hearts of people. They do the 20% that the 80% never think of, and by doing so they leave a significant mark on your life, causing you to go higher and deeper in all you do.

These leaders carry a signature voice that consistently and clearly articulates a person's value and worth, which is what makes them so unique and impactful. So, there really isn't just one short definition of what a "signature voice" is. I believe there are many parts that make up the whole package of someone's signature voice. But, to simplify it, your signature voice is your distinct and unique expression.

DISCOVER GOD'S PURPOSE

Your signature voice plays a big part in discovering God's purpose for your life. It carries in it what you are most passionate about. God brings forth your purpose and calling and intertwines it into your signature voice. It's what God created you for, to release and bring into the world. God uniquely designed and fashioned you for a specific purpose. As you seek to discover what God has purposed for you, you begin to tap into the deep things in your heart that you really love. He begins to show you giftings that lie within you. They are there to help carry out His plan and purpose for your life, and it is all channeled through your signature voice.

PARALYZING FEAR

What are your strongest desires? Many times, your strongest desires are a key that the Lord is giving you insight into the purpose to which He has called you. People often have a difficult time finding their signature voice due to a lack of confidence and underlying fears.

The enemy uses fear to paralyze a person to keep them from fulfilling their purpose in life. Perhaps there were bad experiences in a person's past life where someone belittled them and caused them to shut down. They feel they don't have what it takes. They see no value in themselves; therefore, they toss their creative ideas aside because they feel no one will listen to them. The enemy speaks lies to them, and they buy into the lies. At that point, their voice becomes silent and dreams never come to pass.

God's desire is for you to overcome those fears and step into your calling. He has you and purpose on His mind, and He is fully committed to strengthening you and encouraging you to reach for it.

STRONG DESIRE

Desire is powerful. It's amazing how desire overrides everything. If you have a strong desire, it can overcome fears and impossibilities, and you can do what God has called you to do. Desire will help awaken the greater purpose in you; it is at that point that something inside you knows you cannot stay in the place that

117

never changes. Something has to shift in your life, and you are compelled to give voice to what God has put inside you.

If you hear the enemy telling you that your voice doesn't matter, I encourage you to press on, because your voice does matter. You're called to be a world changer. You're called to impact and influence the world around you. Someone needs to hear what you have to say. They need to hear your wisdom, your insight, your creativity, and your ideas. God will use your voice to bring life to people that are facing difficult and even devastating seasons.

AN ENCOURAGING VOICE

There have been times in my own life that the enemy has tried to keep my voice silent by causing great discouragement so that I would give up and quit. His ultimate goal is to get you to quit so that you will not fulfill your calling.

However, God is so faithful that He will cause an encouraging voice to come across your path. He will set up a divine appointment for you and use someone to speak a powerful word to you that will bring life and infuse you with hope. He will cause someone to prophetically "read your mail" to let you know, He knows right where you are and the challenges you are experiencing.

I will never forget a time when I was overwhelmed with discouragement and disappointment. I went to a meeting, and the Lord used a prophet of God to speak to the giftings and callings within me so precisely. She began to speak forth moments in my future and desires I had in my heart. God showed her these things to bring great encouragement to me so I would stay the course. The things she spoke over me resonated in my spirit so loudly settling me.

They were hidden desires within me that only the Lord and I knew, for He had shown me these things years ago. God knew I was at a place that I needed Him to show up in a specific way. He graciously used this woman to do the job. I'm so grateful this woman of God never gave up on her calling so that she could speak into my life at a time I needed it the most. Your voice matters!

God intricately uses the body of Christ together to fulfill His purpose. Every person carries a supply that brings the completion and fulfillment of a thing. As the word says, every joint supplies (Eph. 4:16). That is why your voice matters. You bring a supply that only you can bring, which will cause others to step into their position and place so that they can fulfill their part.

HOW YOU USE YOUR VOICE

Let there be a grace to you and your voice. Learn to use your voice with grace, yet powerfully for God. I'm continually learning that in my own life and ministry. It's a process as you humble yourself and allow God to refine and sharpen you. The way you use your voice in your delivery is important because it can either engage people or cause them to check out. I have learned in my own life to speak boldly, and deliver truth on a love platter that is easier to receive and digest. Most importantly, submit your voice to God and always endeavor to follow the Holy Ghost and heed His instruction. Be you, but be teachable, quick to make adjustments that are needed to be more effective.

LOSING MY VOICE

One time I caught a cold, which unfortunately affected my voice. For several days, I did not have a voice with which to articulate my thoughts. I had no idea that losing my voice would impact me as much as it did. I suddenly realized how terrible it would be to be unable to articulate my thoughts, as well as being unable to speak out the Word of God. Or to be unable to praise the Lord God Almighty and give Him thanks.

An overwhelming compassion came over me for the mute and those who have lost their voice due to trauma or tragedy because I know the power in giving voice to God's word over circumstances and making decrees. I know the power in making declarations and speaking to mountains, commanding them to move. I know the power in making a decree, especially decreeing the Blessing of God over my family; for it will unlock destiny in their lives! I know the power in giving voice to The Name that is above all names, the mighty matchless name of Jesus. There have been times in my life that in a life or death situation, I knew I had to speak the name of Jesus with my mouth-my voice.

On another occasion, the enemy came after me in my sleep

one night and literally tried to smother me. He took my breath, and I could not breathe. I knew in order to stop the attack and bind that spirit, I had to speak the name of Jesus with authority. I was struggling to get a breath. It seemed like seconds were minutes. Finally, I gasped for air, got a breath and spoke the name of Jesus with every ounce of authority in me, and instantly the spirits left, and the demonic attack was gone! The Spirit of God began ministering to me, unpacking a greater revelation of how powerful the name of Jesus is when spoken with my own voice, and with authority!

How about you? Have there been times that you have experienced some life or death situations? I want to admonish and encourage you to use the name of Jesus. Everything has to bow to that name! Maybe there is a situation in your life that is overtaking you. Or perhaps you have felt a great amount of resistance come against you lately that seems out of the ordinary and more like a demonic attack against you to stop you from stepping into the new. Open your mouth and use the name of Jesus! There is POWER in that name!

YOU NEED A PLACE

Your soul needs a place of rest to step into a place of discovery. Place value on your life and your time. Honor yourself and get away with God because He wants to take you to that place of rest where your soul (your mind, will, and emotions) can begin to breathe in a new way. He wants you to come away with Him to this place so He can cause creativity to come alive in you and help you discover your signature voice and what you're passionate about. I truly believe you have to create margin in your life to get with God and let Him reveal your signature voice to you. When you present yourself to Him and say, "I'm here Lord, I'm ready," the Great Teacher will appear and reveal.

I like to get away in a place of beauty with the Lord. Everything around you affects you. For me, it's important to surround myself with beautiful things, because it affects creativity and the deeper things within me. Finding the environment that is pleasing and beautiful will create an atmosphere and begin to speak to your soul. It opens you up in a way and ignites new things in you. When I get to my place, things I didn't see before ignite and come alive in me. It's in that place where the Lord pulls things out of me and brings clarity and vision.

It's also in that place where you begin to dream. Dream big and get a visual showing you what you're all about. Let that dream and desire rise up large in you. Let it inspire you for more.

POWER OF WORDS

Your signature voice isn't only about your distinct-unique expression and calling, but it carries great power in your life. Your voice knows what belongs to you. That's why it's imperative to give voice to the desires in your heart and create your life.

Words carry great power. Words are important entities that bring tangible things to your life through the power of God. In

Genesis 1, we see that God spoke out what He saw in His mind by saying "Let there be…" He spoke and created the earth, the planets, the sun, the moon and the stars, as well as every animal on the planet, and humanity itself. He saw all of these in His mind, and He spoke and created. He spoke and by His very words, what once was nonexistent became manifested in the physical realm. That's how powerful words can be.

In the book of James, we learn how words, and the power of the tongue, work in our lives.

"For we all stumble and sin in many ways. If anyone does not stumble in what he says [never saying the wrong thing], he is a perfect man [fully developed in character, without serious flaws], able to bridle his whole body and rein in his entire nature [taming his human faults and weaknesses]. Now if we put bits into the horses' mouths to make them obey us, we guide their whole body as well. And look at the ships. Even though they are so large and are driven by strong winds, they are still directed by a very small rudder wherever the impulse of the helmsman determines. In the same sense, the tongue is a small part of the body, and yet it boasts of great things."

JAMES 3:2-5 (AMP)

The captain of a ship is the person who operates the steering gear. He plots out his course to the destination to which he is traveling. The course is created in the pilot's thoughts first, then it's communicated through the rudder, which causes the entire ship to line up in that same direction. That's the picture James is painting here, referring to our words and what we say. Our words, quite literally, steer our lives and frame our world.

POWER IN SPEAKING

It's not enough to know and understand the power of words. The power lies in the speaking. You have power in your voice. There is a force that explodes when you begin to give voice to the Word of God.

Victory has a shout and faith has a voice! It is alive. God's Word is filled with faith and power. You release your faith when you declare the Word of God from your heart, not your head. When you do, it will move mountains!

This truth is stated in 2 Cor. 4:13: "And since we have the same spirit of faith, according to what is written, "I believed, and therefore I spoke," we also believe and therefore speak."

The spirit of faith is contagious! Therefore, it is important to spend quality time with people who have this spirit of faith. They're different. They see things through a different lens with a positive - "we can do it!" perspective. When you hear their words of faith, you come up higher and start to expect supernatural miracles. Just being around them ignites you, and what is on them, rubs off on you!

WHAT IS THE SPIRIT OF FAITH?

What is the spirit of faith? Paul says it is "believing" and "speaking." For the is as crucial as the believing part.

In order to maintain a spirit of faith in your life, you must keep your voice hooked up to your spirit. Otherwise, your voice will hook up with your feelings, emotions, and circumstances. Your thoughts will want to hook your voice up with your intellect and your reasoning. But, you must keep it connected to your spirit to stay in faith.

> *"For verily I say unto you, That whosoever shall say unto this mountain, Be thou removed, and be thou cast into the sea; and shall not doubt in his heart, but shall believe that those things which he saith shall come to pass; he shall have whatsoever he saith. Therefore I say unto you, What things soever ye desire, when ye pray, believe that ye receive them, and ye shall have them."*
>
> MARK 11:23, 24 (KJV)

Your voice knows where you live. I heard someone say one time, "Your voice knows your address." Whatever you speak out of your mouth is what will arrive at your house - good or bad. So, we must be careful with what we speak. We need to hear our voice speak faith-filled words of blessing and life. It makes a difference in everyday life and throughout the years.

When I was a little girl, I learned from my dad to speak God's Blessing over people and to always believe the best in people. He taught me that if there was a will, there was a way - not to let anything stop me and that I had what it takes to make a difference. Both my dad and stepdad taught me that. They both had such a positive outlook towards things and carried a spirit of faith about them and still do to this day. As a little girl, I didn't understand the impact my words would have on people and in my own life. I did not realize what was happening inside of me by just being around them. But, now I see how the spirit of faith that they carried got on me, even as a little girl! It impacted me greatly, affecting what lens I would look through for my life and see all the possibilities in God.

A YEARNING FOR SIGNIFICANCE

As we discussed earlier in this chapter, finding your signature voice is key to be impactful and influential for your purpose and calling. Knowing it is not your voice alone that makes a difference, but it is the entire make-up of your signature voice that sets you apart from others, allowing you to be even more impactful and influential, marking a person's life by truly being the difference and imparting into their heart. The impact is life-changing!

It is a process as I'm still learning myself. However, I know in my heart we can all come to a place of knowing our signature voice so we can run with the dreams God has placed inside our hearts. I truly believe there is a strong desire in every person to find their purpose, significance, and their signature voice in the world. I see that to be true as I have seen it in their eyes whether in America or in other nations that I have traveled to. They yearn for purpose and significance; they are searching for it. They need to be told, "It's in YOU"! They need to be told, "You can make the difference with your signature voice"!

It's in YOU! Own it!

CHAPTER TEN

CALL IT THE WAY GOD SEES IT

O ne Saturday afternoon, on a cool sunshiny day, I had set out for a marathon walk. I love long walks. I love to get outside, breathe the fresh air, look at the beautiful scenery and explore the area. It is one of my favorite things to do, especially when I travel. I particularly love my prayer time with the Lord-praying for my city or the city I'm visiting and praying in things that need to be established in that place. I love that He shows me new discoveries of things I have not seen and ministers to me about them.

This particular day, I was talking to the Lord about some things in my life that were not going the way I thought they should be going. I went on and on telling Him this and that - really complaining in a way. All the sudden, in my spirit I heard,

"Call it the way you want to see it." As you can imagine, that instantly got my attention, and I said, "What Lord?" Then I heard it again, "Call it the way you want to see it." I heard, "Call it the way I see it," the last time.

I know that God created me for His purpose and He has given me power and authority to "Call it the way I want to see it," according to His Word. Paul tells us in Rom. 4:17, "To call those things that be not as though they were."

YOU ARE CREATED FOR GOD'S PURPOSE

We established earlier that God has a destiny etched within you for a people group. He has a purpose and calling for your life. God created purpose before He created man. We talked about how Paul explains in Ephesians 2:10: "For we are his workmanship, created in Christ Jesus unto good works, which God hath before ordained that we should walk in them."

You are His workmanship, which means you are crafted-you are the handiwork of God. Everything about you is purposefully designed with intention for God's purpose. Purpose is the reason you exist. Therefore, everything about you is created for your purpose. Frustration comes when a person isn't walking in their purpose of what God created them to do. Agitation, frustration, and irritation come when you settle for less than your destiny. You sense an inner emptiness because you feel powerless.

The question is, how do you live out your purpose? How do you discover that purpose and the power God has given you to live it out?

130

All of us were created in the image of God to be world changers. God wants to use you to be an agent of change not only for your family, but in your community, and in your work place.

BECOME A WORLD CHANGER

What is a world changer? A world changer is one who advances the Kingdom of God on the earth. Jesus Christ empowered us over two thousand years ago, by reconciling us back to God. He empowered us by giving us the advantage, the authority, and the ability to bring His kingdom here to earth. Thy kingdom come, thy will be done on earth as it is in heaven (Matt. 6:10). God is not only trying to get us to heaven; He is trying to get heaven here on earth.

The question is, do you avail yourself? What can God use you for? Will you allow God to use you to make a difference in the world and be a world changer? Better yet, will you BE the difference in your city? Will you let Him use your voice to bring heaven to earth and call it the way He sees it?

DECREE A THING

"Thou shalt also decree a thing, and it shall be established unto thee: and the light shall shine upon thy ways."

(JOB 22:28) (MSG)

In the Hebrew, decree means to decide, to determine, an enhancement. It is an appointment of space of time, of quality of labor or wage. When we decree a thing, we make a determina-

131

tion and a decision. It begins to speak of something prescribed such as a task or a portion. The verb indicates, to separate, divide, to cut off, to destroy. The primary root tells us that when we make a decision, we are cutting things away. When we make a decree, and it is established, we are deciding what we want, and it will happen. You have to know your purpose before it can manifest. You have to know what you want.

When we decree a thing, or we make a decision, we first cut other things away. There are things in our lives that may not fit anymore. You may be living a life that is not authentic to the value of your voice. It is not what you were designed and created for. That is where frustration can set in because you don't have passion; passion is where you get your power. God designed you for something very specific that no one else on this earth can do but you. As we established earlier, you are called with a specific calling, and it is up to you to discover your purpose and destiny.

When we cut out or let go-in our minds and in our souls-those things that do not belong, it will change the quality of our lives. We are agreeing, or coming into alignment with the decree, the decision, and determination of God. When your spirit, and your agreement, come into agreement with God's decree for your life, something comes alive inside of you. You can then live the abundant life that Christ died to give you according to John 10:10.

God has a plan for you according to Jeremiah 29:11, and that plan is for good and not evil, to prosper you and give you the expected end. God has His whole plan laid out for your life. Are you willing to come into alignment and agree with the decree?

What we want most in life, turns out to be the touchstone of our development. When we ask for love, God will give us troubled people to love and to help. When we ask a favor, God will give us opportunities. Even in crisis moments, God will use those moments to pull something out of you and even birth something new because all things are working for the good of those who love God and are called according to His purpose (Rom. 8:28).

THE CALL INSIDE YOU

There is a call inside of you that carries you to discover, define, and develop inner skills so that you will become skillful and brilliant at what you have been called to do in life. Look what God says to Jeremiah: "Before I formed you in the womb I knew you; Before you were born I sanctified you; I ordained you a prophet to the nations" (Jeremiah 1:5).

This verse applies to you as well. Before you were ever in your mother's womb, God Himself ordained you and called you. He chose you and set you apart. He consecrated you and He already made a decision about you. The Apostle Paul echoes this in Galatians 1:15, "But when it pleased God, who separated me from my mother's womb and called me through His grace."

The word separated in the Hebrew means set off by boundaries or to mark. To appoint means to decree, to declare, to determine, to specify. In other words, God specified you when you were in your mother's womb. That scripture means He clearly intended, He designed, He destined, He defined, He determined, and He decided upon you. If you let that sink in, it will totally liberate you! If God created you, formed you, loved you, and accepted you-just as you are-then the greatest gift you can give yourself is acceptance.

God's decree is your personal destiny. It is your life-long assignment to fall in love with the people your calling gives you access to. He has given you delegated authority to decree a thing, and it will be established, so you can walk in His decrees.

You need to call it the way He sees it concerning you, and you need to call it the way you want to see it. What do you want? What would you like to see? What does God say about you? What does He say about your inheritance?

THE ANOINTING TO DECREE

A prophetic anointing changes the atmosphere. God will put an anointing in your mouth for you to decree a thing so it will be established. He will give you a word to speak. When you give voice to that word to make a decree, the anointing will carry that word to change your atmosphere and situation.

There are times when you may receive a prophetic word. That word carries inherent power to turn the word received into reality released. The ability to perform the word is locked in the Word itself. That is why faith is so important.

"We having the same spirit of faith, according as it is written, I believed and therefore I have spoken; we also believe, and therefore speak;" 2 COR. 4:13 (NKJV)

Revelation causes faith and faith gives us a foundation to speak and decree a thing. First Paul received revelation, then he received faith, and third, he confessed-he spoke.

You have a Signature Voice. There is not another voice like yours. You can decree God's Word over your situation; you begin to call it the way you prophetically see it.

"(As it is written, I have made thee a father of many nations,) before him whom he believed, even God, who quickeneth the dead, and calleth those things which be not as though they were." ROM. 4:17 (NKJV)

To call means to summons; it is to order or request the attendance of. An example would be when a person is summonsed into court to be a witness. The judge uses his power and authority to call for this person's presence and attendance; therefore, they must show up. Likewise, God has given us delegated authority to use His power to call forth things that need to exist according to the Word of God.

The natural realm is an anchor of unbelief, but the spiritual realm is an anchor of hope and faith and full of power. That realm produces the supernatural, which makes all things impossible.

No matter what challenge you are facing today, you can develop the attitude that if God said it in His Word, then it is so in my life. See your situation and your circumstances with the eyes of your spirit and know the battle is already won. It is imperative that we enforce the victory in our lives. We do so by calling things forth and making decrees.

Decreeing the Word of God is the highest authority, it is God's Word that carries the final authority.

"So shall My word be that goes froth from My mouth; It shall not return to Me void, But it shall accomplish what I please, And it shall prosper in the thing for which I sent it." Isaiah 55:11 (KJV)

We are promised that the word we decree will not return void. We can learn more about a decree in the book of Esther:

"Now you write to the Jews as you see fit, in the king's name, and seal it with the king's signet ring; for a decree which is written in the name of the king sealed with the king's signet ring may not be revoked." Esther 8:8 (KJV)

When you make a decree in the name of the king, it cannot be re-written or revoked. That's powerful! That means the decree you make in the name of Jesus cannot be revoked. Wow!

Many people today are using positive affirmations, especially entrepreneurs, professionals, and those in the corporate world. They focus on writing positive things about themselves. They carry an attitude of success through positive affirmations and the law of attraction, but God is not included. People are trying to build themselves up to believe that they can do anything on their own. But many will fall flat, and they can be easily shaken.

What they don't realize is positive affirmation originated in the Word of God. God created it, yet the enemy has taken it, twisted it, and made a counterfeit out of it. There is no solid foundation, or true power backing them. The Word of God is where the power is. The Bible verse 3 John 1:2 demonstrates what some call the law of attraction. It says, "Beloved, I pray that in all respects you may prosper and be in good health, just as your soul prospers." This verse reveals the importance of our soul over every area of our lives. The soul is our mind, our will, and our emotions. Our health, prosperity and the overall well-being of our lives are connected to our minds. There are natural laws of the universe like gravity; God is the Creator of these laws that govern the universe and nature. God's laws work for all peoples at all times whether you are a Christian or not. The law of attraction is like the law of gravity-whatever your thoughts, your habits and your beliefs are going into will create the life you live.

God gave us His authority in the world, and we have the opportunity to partner with Him through our thoughts and the words we speak, and then watch it change our reality. The Word is the final authority, so we need to make it the final authority in our lives because that is where true power comes. When I came to this revelation, it changed my life. It changed not only my belief system and thought life, but it changed how I speak.

When you make a decree, and that decree is made in the name of the King, it cannot be revoked. That word you decree goes out and begins to create for you on your behalf. Immediately, it begins to attract the essence of that word to you. If you create an atmosphere for blessing and speak blessing, blessing will come knocking on your door.

When I started making more decrees in my life, I began to see a significant change in other areas that I had not exercised this principle in yet. We were having some difficulty in the office, so I started making decrees concerning my co-workers and our work atmosphere. I began to create an atmosphere of blessing and speak blessing in that place. I made decrees of blessing over my co-workers and spoke to different situations concerning them like how well we all worked and flowed together. Where there were tension and strife in particular areas, it became peaceful and easy. I changed the way I addressed each person and started speaking to their potential and the nature of Christ inside of them; for how you address people determines the nature that you will call forth out of them. When you do so, you automatically let them know something of your expectation in how you address them, and it calls forth their potential. This principle is literally taking the Word of God in Rom. 4:17 and applying it to specific situations in your life. What a turnaround I saw in attitudes, behaviors, and their ability to work and flow easily together. The atmosphere became a place of peace and enjoyment.

THE AUTHORITY OF THE DECREE

Earlier in this chapter, I mentioned part of what the word decree means. To bring more enlightenment-the word decree in the English definition is very close to what we find in Esther. It is the authority of a court order. If a criminal receives a prison sentence, that criminal has no right to choose whether he goes to prison or not. He has no choice or right in the matter. That is the level of the authority in God's Word.

In the Bible, the word decree includes the purposes of God. It is the weight and authority with the purposes of God behind it. You can always tell when someone's words are anointed; they carry weight and power.

To expound further, the Hebrew definition of the word decree is to separate, divide, to cut off, to destroy. When you are decreeing something, you are separating, cutting off, dividing, and destroying things. For example, when you decree prosperity, not only is it the weight of a court order that cannot be opposed or revoked but also, you are cutting off lack and destroying poverty spirits. It is both of those things at the same time. Wow!

When you decree justice for yourself-or someone else-you are cutting off injustice. It is a true separation. You could say a decree separates the sheep from the goats. A decree separates the goodness of God from the attack of the enemy.

When you really grasp the full meaning behind the word decree, to the point that it becomes part of you, then you will know you are truly sealing the enemy's fate in your life. It is already done; we just have to establish it with our words. That is the key!

It is important that we decree the realm of blessing in our lives and over our family. You establish it by decreeing your realm of blessing with the Word of God. Once you do that, then you need to live within that realm. You are separating yourself and defining your borders unto the goodness and life of God. You need to define your borders and what that land looks like. It should look like, and manifest as the blessings, the goodness, and glory of God.

I have always been captivated with David's life because he was a king and longed for his heart to be one with God's heart. God even said David was a man after His own heart. David was a king; therefore, his decrees could not be revoked. David knew what it meant to stand on the truth of the Word. He knew what it was to stand on the decrees of what God had spoken to his heart; not only was he the king, but he operated with the anointing of a prophet and priest as well.

We find in the book of Psalms, David's words were from his heart, and from a place of such humility, that they carried much weight. He was real and transparent when pouring his heart out to the Lord in his distress, and relaying to God certain facts about things that were happening. Even so, David always ended with a truth and a victory. He always ended on a high note, praising God.

FACTS AND TRUTH

Facts and truths are different. Facts are based on the temporal realm, but truth is based on the unchanging Word of God. Truth cannot be shifted because it's in the eternal realm. The fact is you may have been diagnosed with cancer, but the truth is by His stripes you were healed (1 Pet. 2:24). We, as believers, need to learn to live by the truth about a matter, not the facts. It can become a matter of life and death.

We make a decree and declare a truth that cannot be shifted. That's exactly what David did. He identified the fact about his circumstances at the moment, but he always turned to the truth and lived in the truth. David tapped into a place with God, and the truth about God's love for him. When you read David's writings, he takes you to another level. He takes you to a high place in God where he makes decrees about his life.

Like David, you need to write decrees at the highest level that will create open heaven over your life, your family, your business, your job, your ministry, and your sphere of influence. You need to call it the way you want to see it!

The more you begin to use God's Word to make decrees, the more it will change your thinking. It is the truth, and the power in the scripture going forth that begins to renew your mind. It is important that you renew your mind to the Word of God so that you can open yourself up to the truth, otherwise you are stuck in the fact.

As your words are spoken out, it not only renews your mind and changes your perspective, but it changes the atmosphere and creates a place where an open Heaven can exist. Where God's presence can be present and dwell. It completely changes everything. It is like a magnet when you release the Word of God; it attracts the presence of God Himself and the presence of angels.

It says in Psalm 103:20 (NASB), "Bless the Lord, you His angels, Mighty in strength, who perform His word, obeying the voice of His word!" We have to give voice to God's word. And as soon as we give voice to His word by decreeing and speaking the word, then angels are dispatched.

The Lord upholds His word. He told Jeremiah (my paraphrase), "Jeremiah, you decree the word, but I am watching over My word to perform it" (Jer. 1:12). The moment we give voice to decree the word, God goes to work to perform what we just decreed. Knowing that truth gives me great confidence, and I can enter into a place of rest. I can wait with an expectancy and watch it happen!

In Job 22:28 it says, "You shall decree a thing, and it shall be established for you." In a legal contract, you can maybe do something, or you can do something, or you shall do something. The word shall is required in a contract. The word shall is like a commandment in this verse: you shall make a decree and it SHALL-it MUST be-established for you.

When you see it that way, it will boost your confidence because there is no question about it; it shall be established in your life! If you ever had a doubt, it will be removed from you. The Word of God is clear. He is watching over His Word to perform it. It will not return void!

Not only will the word be established, but the result of that happening will cause God's light to shine upon your way. "... And light will shine on all your ways." The Hebrew meaning of the word light in this verse means, the light of instruction, the light of prosperity, the light of truth, righteousness and integrity. The Hebrew language has so much to reveal in each one of these words. Such rich revelation comes forth.

OUR INHERITANCE

One area that has always been important to me, and very strong on my heart, is my inheritance. It's interesting to see what happens when you begin to decree over your family and your bloodline. The Spirit of God began to show me more of my inheritance, not only my spiritual inheritance but also my family inheritance.

He reminded me of some things I received from my Memaw (my pet name for my grandma), that are very special and dear to my heart. One had to do with her diamond wedding ring, which was an inheritance to me. When I began to wear it and decree over my family, I began to see greater things come forth in my life as well as my family's lives, like honor and reestablishment of family order. Not only that, but the Lord began to bring my siblings spouses establishing family. The Lord ministered to me that He was going to bring my family into a new place of honor, especially my father. That he would be shown honor from some former employees, who had dishonored him in the past. The Lord also showed me that he would receive recognition concerning areas he has been faithfully operating in for years, but had been overlooked. God is always faithful to restore and give honor where honor is due. He also ministered to me that He would reestablish my inheritance and generational things. Things that the enemy stole in the realm of family, God has reestablished and continues to in its fullness. Inheritance that I didn't even know was mine; He has revealed and delivered to my door. Amazing!

The Lord is all about honor, honoring the honorable, and even the dishonorable. I'm reminded of David's covenant agreement with Saul because of his covenant with Jonathan, Saul's son. Jonathan loved David as his own soul the Bible says (1 Sam. 18:1). His soul was knit to David's, for they both had a real relationship with God. After Jonathon heard David share his heart with Saul, he knew he and David had the same heart. When Saul took David in, Jonathan and David made a covenant of friendship that would prove stronger than jealousy, than envy, than ambition. It was a covenant for life.

After Saul died, David asked, "Is there anyone still left of the house of Saul to whom I can show kindness for Jonathan's sake?" (2 Sam. 9:1) David was looking to see if there was anyone in Saul's family that David could bless and honor.

Mephibosheth, who was Jonathan's son (Saul's grandson), didn't know about this covenant, but it was an activated covenant already in place. David called Mephibosheth to come in before him. Then he also called for Saul's steward, Ziba. To Ziba, he gave these instructions regarding Saul's surviving grandson:

> *Then the king summoned Ziba, Saul's steward, and said to him, "I have given your master's grandson everything that belonged to Saul and his family. You and your sons and your servants are to farm the land for him and bring in the*

crops, so that your master's grandson may be provided for. And Mephibosheth, grandson of your master, will always eat at my table." (Now Ziba had fifteen sons and twenty servants.)   II SAMUEL 9:9, 10 (NKJV)

This is a picture of how God takes care of His own. I'm sure there are many people in the world who have had inheritances left to them, but were unclaimed. In the Lord, we can call forth lost inheritance.

You may have had an inheritance coming to you, and something happened to where that has been locked up. In the name of Jesus, I decree a release to you of all that was promised in Jesus' name.

You may need a financial breakthrough in your life. In the name of Jesus, I decree to you that the money you currently have will go further than you could ever imagine it to the natural. I call in multiplication to your household. I say that debts are being forgiven. I call in any money that is owed to you to come to your address, in the mighty matchless name of Jesus.

Lastly, I decree for honor to be restored back to you and your family, and I decree the goodness and blessing of the Lord over you, in Jesus name.

I encourage you to make decrees yourself. Call it the way you want to see it-Call it the way He sees it!

It's in YOU!

CHAPTER ELEVEN

CREATOR CREATING
IN YOU

I love chocolate! One of my favorite chocolate desserts is chocolate cake with chocolate icing. Not just chocolate cake, with chocolate icing, but warm chocolate cake right out of the oven with chocolate icing melting on top! One of my favorite memories at my grandparents home was eating all the delicious desserts that my Memaw would make. The smell of her homemade cookies was luscious, and her homemade chocolate cake was lip-smacking, mouthwatering delicious!

Imagine that in your kitchen right now you have a piece of warm chocolate cake that just came right out of the oven. Can't you just smell the rich chocolate aroma? Picture yourself picking up a fork and cutting into the delicious cake. See yourself taking a bite of the warm, rich chocolate cake and it melting in your mouth. Can you feel yourself salivating-not in your mind's eye, but in "real life"?

Imagination is powerful. Thoughts are powerful. These two definitely flow together. Focus thoughts become images that can take us somewhere that we desire to go. These thoughts start out as dreams, but at some point, they become our actions. These thoughts are filled with what we are passionate about. They motivate us and get us moving to take action.

IMAGINATION IN ACTION

We can imagine something from the beginning of its creation to the result of what we desire. We can see it already completed before we even begin to start it. The Bible says that God sees the end from the beginning (Is. 46:10). He not only sees the end from the beginning, but He sees everything in between. God created the world, and He saw it from beginning to the end.

In Genesis 11, we see the power of imagination in action.

Now the whole world had one language and a common speech. As people moved eastward, they found a plain in Shinar and settled there.

> *They said to each other, "Come, let's make bricks and bake them thoroughly." They used brick instead of stone, and tar for mortar. Then they said, "Come, let us build ourselves a city, with a tower that reaches to the heavens, so that we may make a name for ourselves; otherwise we will be scattered over the face of the whole earth."* GEN. 11:1-4 (NKJV)

At that point, the Lord came down to see the city and the tower the people were building.

The Lord said, "If as one people speaking the same language they have begun to do this, then nothing they plan to do will be impossible for them. Come, let us go down and confuse their language so they will not understand each other."
So the Lord scattered them from there over all the earth, and they stopped building the city. That is why it was called Babel-because there the Lord confused the language of the whole world. From there the Lord scattered them over the face of the whole earth. GEN. 11:5-9 (NKJV)

We see that everyone on earth spoke the same language at one point. They began to imagine building a city and a tower for themselves. In verse 6, God made a very interesting statement. He said that nothing would be restrained from them, which they have imagined to do.

Now evidently, God didn't want them doing this; therefore, He put a stop to it. But, we need to grasp that these people dreamed and imagined that they could build a city and a tower. They were in agreement; they were of one mind and one accord. Their imagination became very powerful when they were corporately focused together.

THE IMAGE OF YOUR FUTURE

Hopes and dreams are images of our future. They sustain us and keep us steady until they come to pass. We need these powerful images inside of us to keep us moving through the process while we are waiting for the fulfillment of that dream to come. During the waiting process, the enemy will always bring challenging situations and circumstances with the purpose to abort those dreams.

This reminds me of one of my favorite scriptures: "I would have lost heart unless I had believed that I would see the goodness of the Lord in the land of the living" (Psalm 27:13). This verse has kept me steady throughout different seasons and brought hope when my surroundings and situation did not look at all promising.

ABRAHAM'S IMAGINATION

God promised Abraham a son, but it took 25 years of waiting for his promise, Isaac, to be born. God told Abraham that his descendants would enter the Promised Land, but that didn't happen for several centuries. There will always be a delay between the promise and the provision, but God always delivers right on time. His timing is perfect. Our job is to be like Abraham-fully persuaded God is able to perform the promise in our life. "And being fully persuaded that, what he had promised, he was able also to perform." (Rom. 4:21) Are you fully persuaded about what God has promised and spoken to you?

Whenever we are fully persuaded, it means that we are carried by what we have heard. We heard a word from God, we believed it was God, and we are carried by this thing even when circumstances begin to defy it. When God gives you a prophetic promise-a prophetic word, you walk on the power of that word. You are sustained by the power of that word. When God says, "Live," even a dead person can come back to life. There is power in that word He spoke, and so you begin to walk fully persuaded just by the power of that word He spoke, which in turn will literally carry you. You are carried by the word you heard God say to you.

There is a strengthening that you know God will fully carry out His word and His will for your life which He has already spoken or revealed to you. When you hear something, and you are fully persuaded by that thing, you will be quickened in your spirit if you believe it. You will be fully persuaded that God is talking to you and that it is true. Abraham was fully persuaded that God was talking to him and that what He said was true so much so, that it formed a powerful image inside of him that helped carry him through to the promise.

God will speak a promise to you at a time when circumstances totally defy and look like the opposite of what God is saying. He will prophesy to you that you will be blessed when you're struggling to pay your bills. But, God already sees you blessed and in a wealthy place. He will call you healed when you're sick in your body with pain. He will call you whole when you are still broken. He will call you a mighty man or woman of valor even though you don't see yourself that way. You must be fully persuaded and carried by that word which you heard from Him. Even when all the circumstances are denying it, even when it has caused such a delay to the degree that it is making you look like it will never come to pass and you almost lose hope. You have to go back like Abraham and be carried by the word that God gave you in the beginning.

Abraham was carried by the word God spoke to him. Even though there was a delay, Abraham was fully persuaded by the word God spoke, and that word carried him through into his promise land. Abraham laid hold of the hope set before him.

> *For men indeed swear by the greater, and an oath for confirmation is for them an end of all dispute. Thus God, determining to show more abundantly to the heirs of promise the immutability of His counsel, confirmed it by an oath, that by two immutable things, in which it is impossible for God to lie, we might have strong consolation, who have fled for refuge to lay hold of the hope set before us. This hope we have as an anchor of the soul, both sure and steadfast.* HEB. 6:18-19 (NKJV)

Hope is the anchor for our soul. Hope will come to us in an inner image giving us a vision of what God has in mind for us. These images have the power to sustain us through the delays and the most challenging difficulties. In Romans 4:18, Paul said this about Abraham: "…who, contrary to hope, in hope believed, so that he became the father of many nations, according to what was spoken, So shall your descendants be."

In other words, against all human hope, pertaining to what could be seen with the natural eye, Abraham held fast to the inner image of God's promise that he saw in his spirit. It was a

God-given dream that sustained Abraham and anchored his soul until the promise came to pass in his life.

JOSEPH'S DREAMS

Just as God used imaginations, hopes, and dreams in Abraham's life, he also did the same in Joseph's life. God gave Joseph many dreams as a young man. Those dreams created inner images in Joseph that revealed promotion, authority, and power that would come to pass later in Joseph's life. Joseph faced challenges and setbacks, but in his imagination, he saw his dreams of authority and held fast to them.

Throughout the years, God has given me many dreams that not only encouraged me but sustained me through many waiting seasons. Numerous times, He would give me a dream of several different people whom I highly esteemed and admired. In these dreams, I would sit down with them over coffee, and we would visit. They did most of the talking, and I did the listening. It was like a mentorship of them pouring wisdom and instruction into me, giving me insight on many things that I had not experienced yet.

Upon awakening from these dreams, I was always so encouraged and strengthened to stay the course and continue with what He had put before me. They would also stretch my imagination and create inner images in me because God would show me things in my dreams that I would be doing in the future-preaching, singing, traveling to the nations to minister, and writing.

God has used these dreams to show me detailed specifics of my destiny, areas of promotion that would come into my life-many which have come to pass, and more to come. How exciting it is when you see them come to pass?

The dreams would come at a critical time when I was struggling with frustration or perhaps even disappointment. These dreams greatly strengthened me and brought great hope in my life. I would wake up a new woman with such a spirit of faith inside believing once again that all things are impossible!

YOUR IMAGINATION AND DREAMS FOR THE FUTURE

God will give you imaginations that will speak of His plan for your life. He will show you things and reveal things to you concerning your future. Those create a powerful image inside of you to help you stay the course. They help you press through while infusing you with hope to carry you into your promise land. God will use dreams, visions, and imaginations to fuel your faith through the delays you will encounter as you travel toward your destiny. They will sustain your faith through the challenges that will arise.

MEDITATION PLUS IMAGINATION

As you can see, imagination is a powerful thing, and meditation helps to produce an imagination. What we meditate on, we will imagine. Our imagination has the ability to create. Through our imagination, we are able to create, which in turn can bring forth greater opportunities in life. Imagination is a door that opens a world of possibilities. If you can imagine it, you can believe it and receive it.

Meditate on seeing yourself doing more and being more. Possibilities in your life will change when your perspective changes. When you imagine yourself being more, vision comes alive in you, and you begin to think progressively. Mental images of future possibilities will manifest in your mind, thoughts, and imagination.

Helen Keller once said, "The greatest tragedy in life is people who have sight but no vision." If you don't see it on the inside, you will never see it on the outside. When you read the Word of God, allow the words to form images inside of you so that you can see it on the inside. When you see it on the inside and imagine it, then give voice to what you see, and you will create.

CREATE YOUR FUTURE

God has already given us the power to create our future. We are to follow His example. God spoke, and He created the world and all the fullness that is. When He spoke, He brought the things that already existed in the spiritual realm, into the natural realm by the power of His spoken Word. The Spirit of God lives in you. The Word made flesh-the spirit of Christ Jesus-lives inside of you. It's the Spirit of God in us that teaches us, gives us understanding, insight, and revelation of what already exists in the spiritual realm (John 16). He inspires us with God ideas.

SKILLFUL IN THOUGHT AND SPEECH

Your life is framed by your thoughts and your speech; your life becomes what your thoughts are. This is why you must become skillful in your thoughts and your speech. As you become a master of your thoughts and speech, you will walk fully into your destiny, and you will possess the land God has for you JAMES 3:8 (NKJV)

In a very trying time in my life, the Lord began to deal with me concerning my thoughts and speech. He ministered to me that my life was not going to change and go in the direction I wanted it to until my thoughts were reeled in and my speech changed. God is looking out for us so closely that He will go to lengths for you to get the point so that you can begin to implement it. I recall a day when I was really struggling with this; I open up my emails to notice an email from a minister friend of mine that I highly esteem. He wanted to share with me a new teaching he just put together on your thought life and your words. Wow! Was God getting the message to me or what?

Paul gives us instruction to take every thought captive.

For though we live in the world, we do not wage war as the world does. The weapons we fight with are not the weapons of the world. On the contrary, they have divine power to demolish strongholds. We demolish arguments and every pretension that sets itself up against the knowledge of God, and we take captive every thought to make it obedient to Christ. 2. COR. 10:3-5 (NKJV)

FEAR OR FAITH?

Every battle begins first in your mind; therefore, every battle is won or lost in the mind/thought arena. How we see ourselves is determined in our mind. Do you see yourself strong, influential, and full of the power of God? Or do you see yourself as weak, small, and inferior? The ten Israelites spies saw themselves as weak and small (Num. 13:33). But there were two of the spies-Joshua, and Caleb-who saw themselves differently. These two had a different spirit; they saw the circumstances through the eyes of faith. These two men were set apart because they saw something in their hearts and were ready to reach for more. They believed they were well able to take the land and that they could certainly conquer it (Num. 13:30).

What set Joshua and Caleb apart from the crowd? They obeyed when God said, "Don't let this word depart from your mouth, but meditate upon it day and night" (Josh. 1:8). When you meditate on the Word of God, it strengthens you. It becomes a part of your heart and mind, and eventually, you will speak it out. It becomes a part of who you are because the Word is a living entity. The power that is in the word changes your thoughts.

For the word of God is quick, and powerful, and sharper than any two-edged sword, piercing even to the dividing asunder of soul and spirit, and of the joints and marrow, and is a discerner of the thoughts and intents of the heart.

HEB. 4:12 (NKJV)

157

When your mind thinks what God thinks, and your mouth speaks what God's Word says, faith and hope come alive in your heart. As a result, you can be strong and courageous for the assignment(s) God has given you.

LIFE FOLLOWS THOUGHTS

According to Prov. 23:7, "As a man thinks in his heart so is he." Over the course of our life, we become the sum-total of our thought life. The deepest desires of our heart will drive our will and our actions. Your thoughts build your life. If your thoughts are inferior, then your life will be inferior. If your thoughts are honorable and lofty, then your life will follow, and you will live accordingly.

Whatever we focus on will develop in our life. Whatever we give our attention to, we will become. When people choose to focus on the negative situations in their life, then reoccurring problematic cycles form strongholds in their lives. We have to choose to focus on the positive. It truly is a training and discipline that goes on with your mind and your thought-life.

Finally, brethren, whatsoever things are true, whatsoever things are honest, whatsoever things are just, whatsoever things are pure, whatsoever things are lovely, whatsoever things are of good report; if there be any virtue, and if there be any praise, think on these things. PHIL. 4:8 (KJV)

Whatever is going on in your life is a result from what is happening inside of you. It is a result of your heart and what you're focusing on in your mind. In order to change your life, you have to change your focus and allow God to change your heart. The heart of the matter is always the matter of the heart.

God taught Abraham to focus on the bigger thing that he had for him. He told him to lift up his eyes and look to the north, the south, the east, and the west; that was the land that God was giving to Abraham and his descendants forever. God told him to walk all the land and imagine it as his own because he was going to give it to him.

God was training Abraham to use his imagination and to focus on the big future that he had for him. He was training him to think God-thoughts, which were bigger thoughts than his own. God was training Abraham how to get a vision of something so he could walk into it and live it out.

Years ago, when God began to speak to me concerning ministry, He took me to a big women's conference in Dallas, TX, not only to hear and receive the Word but to help me begin to dream and see the bigger picture of my future and destiny. He wanted to seed me with vision inside so I could begin to walk into it and live it out the rest of my life. It was another monumental moment in my life that moved me into a place with God to set my face like flint-to study and exercise greater discipline in my life for the calling on my life. That defining moment painted an image inside me that I will never forget and has carried me through some very difficult and challenging seasons. That image has helped me fix my focus in order for some things to come to pass in my life, in which I have stepped into them in God's timing.

FOCUS ON THE POSITIVE

In order to change your future, you will have to stop giving place to negativity in your life. Stop focusing on circumstances and situations around you that are limiting you. Stop focusing on things, people, or situations that are smaller than what your heart desires. Purpose in your heart to think positive, intentional thoughts. Begin to think beyond your life and your world. God not only wants to use you where you currently reside, but He wants to expand you to the nations. Think BIG. Think GRAND!

In order for us to be successful and walk in the spiritual blessings that God has for us according to Eph. 1:3, we have to govern our thoughts and meditate daily on His Word. We have to let His Word fill our minds to the point that His thoughts become our thoughts.

KNOWLEDGE OF THE WORD

We must have knowledge of the Word otherwise we won't know what belongs to us. We won't know what is truth. If we don't know what is truth, then our belief system will be incorrect. Jesus said in Mark 9:23, "If you can believe, all things are possible to him who believes." You have to know what the Word says so that you can believe for what God says you can have.

*And be not conformed to this world: but be ye transformed
by the renewing of your mind, that ye may prove what is
that good, and acceptable, and perfect, will of God.*

ROM. 12:2 (KJV)

God's Word has the power to renew our minds. Knowledge
of God's Word teaches us who you are in Christ, and reveals all
the spiritual blessings that He has for us. You must understand
who you were created to be. You were created to be a child of
God-to be His representative. You are His ambassador here on
the earth. Knowing who you are in Christ is one of the most
foundational revelations you have to build on.

As you follow God and let His Word fill your mind and
heart, you will begin to discover all the possibilities in Him. You
will see possibilities and opportunities all around you. You must
keep your focus on the Word, and keep your inner thoughts in
check; otherwise, you'll become a slave to various situations and
circumstances in your life. Those circumstances will control you
and direct your life in a way that you won't want to go. If cir-
cumstances-the storms in your life-are in control they will take
you down a path that leads to distraction and death.

God says in Hos. 4:6, "My people are destroyed for lack of
knowledge: because thou hast rejected knowledge." Don't be left
in the dark and be separated from the abundant life that Jesus
died for to give you. Don't be ignorant of the things of God -
don't be ignorant of the enemy's devices. For the enemy comes
to steal, kill, and destroy, but God comes to bring life and life

more abundantly (John 10:10).

Having the understanding darkened, being alienated from the life of God through the ignorance that is in them, because of the blindness of their heart. Eph. 4:18 (NKJV)

Do not allow the enemy to keep you in the dark. Be in the know of all the spiritual blessings that God has for you. Do not allow him to distract you.

DISTRACTIONS

Distraction leads to the destruction of your dream. Whenever we get distracted, your dream is about to be derailed. A distraction is a ploy to lure you away from doing what you should be doing. When God gives you an assignment, the devil plots a strategy against it to get you to avoid your assignment. Whenever you avoid the assignment and the battle you were born for, you will face another battle you are not equipped for.

You have to stay focused so you can stay in your lane-the place God has called you to and the position He has placed you in. When God spoke prophetically to His people, He would say, "Walk upright, turn neither to the right or the left" -in other words, "Don't be distracted." Be mindful and walk wisely because distractions are subtle, and the devil knows just what to use for each person to distract them.

Distraction has a purpose-its purpose is to distract you from your purpose. Purpose is what you're born for. Everything God does, He does with purpose, on purpose, and for a purpose.

He created us for purpose. Doing the purpose will always cause some level of pain in your life. When we encounter pain, we are looking for a way to have the pain anesthetized because we don't want to hurt. But, the absence of pain is relief, not fulfillment. Do not settle to be relieved, go for fulfillment!

ENLARGING YOUR IMAGINATION

The Spirit of God can inspire us and give us witty inventions according to Prov. 8:12: "I wisdom dwell with prudence, and find out knowledge of witty inventions." God wants to enlarge your imagination. He has good things for you and is up to something good for you. It is far more than you could ever ask, hope, think, dream or imagine according to Eph. 3:20 (MSG). "God can do anything; you know-far more than you could ever imagine or guess or request in your wildest dreams!"

Trust in the Lord with all thine heart; and lean not unto thine own understanding. In all thy ways acknowledge him, and he shall direct thy paths. PROV. 3:5-6 (KJV)

As you acknowledge God in all your ways, thoughts, ideas, and even images will come into your mind. If you acknowledge God in all your ways, and you desire to think His thoughts, then don't discount the thoughts, ideas, and imaginations that come to you. I believe it is the Spirit of God giving you an image inside of you of what He wants to do through you.

I'm reminded of a man who tapped into the power of imagination and vision, and used them to change the world. That man was Walt Disney. He transformed animation from a novelty to an art form. He summarized his creativity in one word: Imagineering. The term Imagineering combines the words imagination and engineering. Imagineering enabled him to transform the dreams and wishes of his imagination into concrete reality-Disney World and Disneyland.

If you want to move forward and progress in life, you have to think progressive thoughts and tap into your God-given imagination. A God-given imagination can create and transform the world around you.

We must become the visionary of our life. Start thinking beyond where you are so that you can reach for more. Take the limits off your mind so you can think outside the box. As you open your heart and mind, God can download divine, creative thoughts, ideas, and imaginations to you. God wants to enlarge your capacity, not just in your thinking, but that's where He will start.

THE PRAYER OF JABEZ

Jabez called on God and asked him to enlarge his borders. Jabez prayed, and God granted him his request. At my home church, The Calling Church in Norman Oklahoma, every Sunday my pastors have the congregation say the prayer of Jabez.

Now Jabez called on the God of Israel, saying, "Oh that You would bless me indeed and enlarge my border, and that Your hand might be with me, and that You would

*keep me from harm that it may not pain me!" And God
granted him what he requested.*   I CHRON. 4:10 (KJV)

This verse came alive in me; I began to give voice to it and
decree it so in my life, as I asked the Lord to enlarge my borders.
I have truly seen this verse work in my life, and effectual doors
have opened. As I mentioned earlier, throughout the years, God
has given me many dreams that created an image inside me concerning my future to hold fast to. These dreams have encouraged
me over the years to keep pressing forward, to hold fast and to
not give up on the dream.

I encourage you to not give up on your dreams. Tap into the
power of imagination and let God do new things in you. Let
your requests be made known to Him, decree and declare those
out daily. He will grant them to you just like He did Jabez. In
doing so, your destiny will be altered, and God will move you
into bigger and greater things for your life.

───────────────

CHAPTER TWELVE

VISION CREATES DESTINY

DESIGNED FOR GREATNESS

God has created you for a purpose. He has fashioned you and designed you for greatness, not just ordinary. No. You have been designed and called for greatness. God has a destiny for you, and His Word says you were destined to reign and succeed.

God has designed us to dream and be creative. He has designed us to be visionaries. He has created us with an incredible mind, with an imagination to dream big dreams. People with vision are continually stirred on the inside with thoughts of purpose waiting to be executed. They're always looking and expecting opportunities to present themselves so they can seize them. People who carry vision not only carry destiny inside them but they cause vision and God's destiny to come alive in others. They are influential in the places God has placed them, and often even extending out to the nations of the world. Vision will show you a picture inside of you that beckons you to step out of yourself and step into what God has shown you in your heart.

Every vision that God gives you is born out of a burden He has shown you in your heart. Until you have a burden, you don't have the capacity to receive a vision. Your vision comes out of your burden. What breaks your heart? What hurts you? What frustrates you? It has to deal with something inside of you, and it is out of that that God will begin to birth a vision. Vision is what you see; the mission is something you do about what you see.

DREAM BIG

God wants you to step outside yourself today-to step outside your limitations, your small thinking, your current resources and finances, your abilities, and your boundaries, to explore and dream the impossible. That's what God wants to do in your life-the impossible! The Word of God says all things are possible with God. Those things that are not possible with man are possible with God Almighty!

God wants to put a dream and a vision inside you to help you fulfill your destiny. Once God awakens the dream and gives you a vision on the inside, you need practical steps to help you execute and carry out the plan.

When you ask God what your purpose is, He will explode

a passion inside you about something. Something will burn in you. You will think about it all the time. It will never leave your thoughts. If you try to run from it, it will come back. You will not be able to shake it. You may try to do something else, but you keep coming back to that thing that caused you to burn inside. This is because you will never find complete fulfillment until you do what God has called you to do. Why? Because He has pre-destined you. He has a plan and purpose for your life. You are not here by accident. You are important and special to Him.

MY AWAKENING

Before I surrendered my life to Jesus, I came to a time in my life where I was miserable. I was searching for real purpose. I tried many things in the world and nothing fulfilled me. Even in all my achievements, I never found full satisfaction and nothing was ever enough. I was searching for greater purpose and significance. I knew deep down in me what I was doing was not what I was called to do. I wanted to know what my purpose was on earth. I thought, There has got to be more to life than this.

In my desperate state, I cried out to God and said, "If you are really alive, and if you are really God, then show Yourself to me and change my life." He answered that prayer!

I had such an encounter with the Living God that it blew me away. He began to show me what He created me for. He revealed to me His plan and purpose for my life. It was at that point that God began to seed me with His dream for my life. He showed me my destiny through dreams and books, through ministers as they spoke, and through people He sent across my path. I spent time with God, and I allowed myself time to dream. I was willing to reach for more if He would only show me. He did, and I began to run towards it, and I'm still running in it today!

YOUR DESTINY; YOUR VISION

Once you know your purpose, you need a vision for your destiny. Destiny is not fate. It's not something that just happens to you or something that's going to happen to you no matter what. No, you are the architect of your life. You have a free will, and you have choices that you can make that will determine your future. This is what puts you in the driver's seat. God will cause opportunities and divine appointments to come across your path, but if you don't seize those opportunities when they come, nothing will happen. Certain things have to come into line, and then you have to take ownership over what is yours. If you don't, you will lose it.

Choices in life make a difference, but nothing happens without thoughts. That's why your thought life and what you focus on is so very important. What you focus on develops in your life. What will you do with the good thoughts, ideas, and concepts God has given you in a dream? This is where vision comes in. You need to take those thoughts that you believe is God-revealed and pray them out. Ask God to give you a vision for them. The Bible says in Prov. 29:18, "Where there is no vision the people perish, but he that keeps the law, happy is he."

You must have a vision for the dream. Without a vision, things will die. Anything that is dying in your life-maybe it's your marriage, your career, your money, or your ministry-it could be for lack of vision. Where there is no vision, things die.

Everyone needs a vision for their family, future, ministry, calling, career. A vision or a dream is a God-inspired expectation that God plants in seed form in the heart of a person. He then makes it visible in their imagination-in their heart. Sight is a function of the eyes, but vision is a function of the heart. The purer the heart, the purer the vision and the clearer you will see it.

In other words, you have to see it. You have to perceive it in order to receive it. If you can see the invisible, you can do the impossible. Vision is a mental picture of a future state. It means to gaze at mentally. It means to perceive. God puts an internal picture inside of you that is bigger than anything outside of you. That's your vision.

That is why the enemy wants to steal your dream. He tried to steal Joseph's dreams. His brothers plotted to get rid of him.

"Here comes that dreamer!" they said to each other. "Come now, let's kill him and throw him into one of these cisterns and say that a ferocious animal devoured him. Then we'll see what comes of his dreams." GEN. 37:19, 20 (NKJV)

What they were actually saying was, what will become of his destiny? Your dream is your destiny, and it needs vision to survive and thrive. With no vision, your dream and your destiny will die.

To take that vision from a dream to the manifestation of reality you must understand,

" the past can teach you

" the present is an opportunity for you, and

" the future is not to be feared.

SEE THE FUTURE STATE

Helen Keller was once asked this question: "What would be worse than being blind?" She replied, "To have sight without vision."

There are people who have natural eyes, but they have no vision. Because they have no vision, everything around them is dying, and that is not the will of God.

God wants you to be able to see, but you will not see it with natural eyes. He wants you to see with spiritual eyes. We walk by faith and not by sight (2 Cor. 5:7). We walk by what God has shown us on the inside, not what we see in the natural.

See your situation by the desired future state that God has promised. It is important that you grasp this. You see it, and it becomes the purpose in your life. God never talks to you according to your current condition. He sees into the future. He called Gideon a mighty man of valor. He said you are not the coward sitting in the wine press, but a mighty man that I've called you to be (Judges 6:12).

God speaks to you according to your destined state, not according to your current condition. Through the Spirit of God, you are able to see. A vision will be made clear to you-not by natural eyesight, but by the eyes of your Spirit. That is why it is imperative for you to have a relationship with the Holy Spirit because He is the One that gives you revelation. He lives inside of you and is with you everywhere you go.

Whenever you have set a vision in your life, there are things that will pop up on your journey.

Vision helps you walk out the purpose God has called you for. It is your future-your destiny. Without a vision, you don't have a future. You need to be a visionary. You need to look ahead to see what all God has for your destiny. Vision is the bridge that takes you from your present into your future. Once you have a clear vision, you will need a strategy to bring that into reality. The strategy is the practical side.

CLARITY AND BOUNDARIES

When you create boundaries, order comes to your life. You can't just pray for order; you must clarify the boundaries. It is important to have clarity on your purpose and assignment. When you don't know where you're going, any road can take you there. Clarity helps you to gain confidence when you are clear on who God called and destined you to be so you can run with your vision.

Clarity helps you to lay a foundation for longevity in your

life. It helps you say "yes" quickly, and it helps you to say "no" gracefully. If it is not about your call, focus, and assignment, then you can say no gracefully. You are not supposed to go through every open door. You have to have clarity, wisdom, and discernment. How do you gain clarity, alignment, and boundaries? You must ask questions, and the Spirit of God will show you.

THE WINNING STRATEGY

You may ask, how do I have the marriage that God has promised? How do I have the family God has promised me? How do I walk into my dreams and destiny that God has put on the inside of me? How do I become blessed and live the abundant life that God promised me? This verse lays out the strategy.

Write down the revelation and make it plain on tablets so that a herald may run with it. For the revelation awaits an appointed time; it speaks of the end and will not prove false. Though it lingers, wait for it; it will certainly come and will not delay. HABAKKUK 2:2-3 (NKJV)

1. Write the vision. That is your action plan or your mission statement.

2. To make it plain; define your goals and objectives clearly.

3. That he may run that reads it. You should develop a team for your vision or your mission statement.

4. That he may run that reads it. You have to implement it.

YOUR ACTION PLAN

Your vision is your mission statement. Develop a statement of purpose. This is a clear picture of what you see and want to achieve.

" Who

" What

" Why

" Where

You must ask yourself these questions and come to the defining moments in your life. You must come to the understanding that God has an assignment and a destiny for you to fulfill. He has much more for your life than for you to just take up space and time.

You were purposed and planned in the mind of God to succeed and achieve great things. You are precisely and purposefully put together by Almighty God. According to Ps. 139:14, you are fearfully and wonderfully made.

You must come to these defining moments in your life because without them, you will spend a lifetime wandering in a wilderness. Many people are frustrated because they don't know who they are and they don't know where they're going. They're settling for less than their destiny.

You are not what your past says you are. You are who God says you are. Your mission statement becomes your reason for existence. Your mission statement is your message.

What is your message for your family, your business, your ministry, your finances, for yourself? You are the message. Everything you do sends a sermon and preaches a message. You are the Living Epistle read of all men. From the way you talk to the way you dress-it is your mission statement, your message. You must define it.

DEFINE YOUR GOALS

Next, you must make it plain and clearly define your goals and objectives. Luke 19:10 tells us that the Son of man has come to seek and save that which was lost. That is the purpose of Jesus.

In Matt. 9:35, we see that Jesus went about all the cities and villages teaching in their synagogues and preaching the Gospel of the Kingdom, healing every sickness and every disease of the people. These are His goals

Goals are bite-size pieces of your vision that can be measured and obtained. The vision of Jesus' destiny was to seek and save that which was lost, but his goals were: I'm going into every city and every village, preaching the Gospel and healing all manner of sickness.

It is a step-by-step process. If you have no goals, your vision will never come to pass. There must be action steps that are measurable and attainable in your life. Without goals, a vision never goes beyond being a dream. Without goals, you will never fulfill your destiny.

God wants more for you than just a dream; He wants to manifest that dream in your life so you can fulfill your destiny and bring you into that place of fulfillment. This is why God says to wait for it. Though it tarries, it shall come to pass. You have to map your success and approach each step as a separate mission; attaining and realizing that your goals will become your vision, which then become your reality. Don't take it on all on at once.

DEVELOP A TEAM

Clearly define your goals and develop a team to run with the dream. The dream does not do the work alone. A vision needs support. Find those who are hungry for what you are hungry for. Find those people who cause your dream to leap inside you, like Mary and Elizabeth. When they came around each other, what was inside them both began to leap (Luke 1:41).

Surround yourself with people who stimulate your dream. Those who are like-minded and have a cause with a passion, because passion is the motivating force. You have to be passionate about your dream, and find those who are passionate with you to develop that team.

Jesus found hungry people, and He was passionate. Not everyone received Him; not everyone wanted what He had. But, that did not stop Him from His purpose. Be passionate about your marriage. Be passionate for your children. Raise them in the way they should go; otherwise, the world will get them. Be passionate about the call on your life, because it is the motivating force that enables you to do what God has called you to do.

People buy into the leader more than they buy into the vision. In other words, it is you they buy into and follow. As you keep the vision before them, it becomes contagious, and you communicate it to them. Teamwork makes the dream work!

IMPLEMENT IT-TAKE ACTION

After you write the vision (your mission statement, goals, and objectives, and developed a team), then you must implement it. Be a doer of the Word and not a hearer only (James 1:22). Faith without works is dead (James 2:20). Faith and works together will conceive your promise. You must take action.

God uses opportunities to increase and advance you. Never let an opportunity pass you by when you know it is a God-opportunity. Be bold and courageous to step through that door and take that opportunity because it may never pass by again. The enemy will try to detour you with enticing opportunities that will lead you down a path of destruction and despair. But, do not fear, for the Spirit of God will show you what He has for you and will lead you by a "perfect peace" within. He will lead you by that inward witness-the still, small voice.

As you follow the leading of the Spirit and take that step of faith into the new, you must stay focused. In all we do, we must stay focused. The devil will try anything to get you off focus. Keep your eye on the prize. The Bible says in Phil. 3:14, "We must press toward the mark for the prize of the high calling of God." You are a person of destiny on your way to happen!

It's in YOU!

CHAPTER THIRTEEN

ENLARGING ON THE INSIDE

God is purposeful in all that He does. He is purposeful in building things inside of you for His glory. His purpose is to build things in you because He has a plan that you are destined and called to.

Do you know what you are called to bring forth in your lifetime? What are you called to change? We inevitably start out in our life-journey with our plans in mind. Then, somewhere along the way, we have an encounter with Christ when we come to the end of ourselves. We surrender to His will and His way and begin to seek Him for His purpose and plan for our lives. We seek to find out what He has destined for us to do. We begin to ask, "What is His calling for my life?"

DARK SEASONS

In our pursuit to find out, we start on a journey to find our-selves-to find out who we really are. Throughout that journey, we experience mountaintop experiences, as well as valley experiences. In those valley times, we can experience some dark seasons when it feels like God is not with us. Rest assured, it is in those times that God will do some of His deepest work in you. He will build things inside of you. You may be in that dark season right now and wonder where God is and what He is doing?

You need to understand that in that dark place, God has His hand on you. What God is doing in you is far greater than what the devil is trying to do to you. God is working a mighty work in you for His glory. He is building something in you to build something out of you. There are hidden treasures that God has for you. The greatest treasures of the kingdom are always hidden just as the greatest treasures on the earth are hidden. Whether it is gold, diamonds, rubies, sapphires-these are hidden. There are hidden treasures inside of you. This is a place where God impregnates you. He is going to do for you what He says in Isaiah 45:3: "I will give you the treasures of darkness and hidden riches of secret places, that you may know that I, the Lord, who calls you by your name, Am the God of Israel."

I prophesy to you, that in this dark season God is giving you your greatest treasures that, until now, have been hidden away for you. He is revealing to you who you are. This is not a time for you to feel God is not working. Relax and let God do in this season what you can't do for yourself.

While you're resting, God is going to open you up and cause something new to come alive in you. He is going to bring something out of you that you didn't even know was in there. He is building things in you because He is going to build something out of you.

God formed Adam, but He built Eve. God has formed something in your life, but there is something in your dark season that God is opening you up to. God is doing such a great work in you. You can be confident of this-He who began a good work in you will perfect it and carry it to completion (Phil. 1:6). There are hidden treasures inside of you.

The Apostle Paul started his journey with the Lord after God revealed His Son to him. Saul of Tarsus, as Paul was first known, was riding his high horse with his plans and purposes to Damascus. Suddenly a light shone around him from heaven (Acts 9:3). That was a divine interruption when God revealed His Son to him. But later in Saul's journey, God revealed Christ in him when God blinded Saul's life in a dark season.

You may not fully understand the revelation of Christ in you. You may quote the scriptures, but it, as ye, has not become revelation knowledge. It has not become Rhema in your life. Rhema means it becomes alive in you and you get revelation on it. I believe you are coming to a breakthrough moment where God is going to open you up and reveal His Son IN YOU.

Jesus loved you and gave His life for you, even when you didn't know who you really were (2 Cor. 5:21). Your identity is found in Him.

Whatever God has called you to, He will lead you through. There may be circumstances that you are facing in your life, and you can't see God in them. He is not hiding from you. God is bringing you to a place where He gives you a song in the night. A song deep within you will rise up in your night season, so when you wake up, you will be satisfied. You will break through into a whole new day with His perception and plan. David sums it up in Ps. 17:15: "As for me, I shall see Your face in righteousness; I will be [fully] satisfied when I awake [to find myself] seeing Your likeness."

You are going to wake up looking like the real you. You will wake up with a revelation of who God has made you to be and what He has placed inside of you.

BUILDING THINGS IN YOU

God wants you to get grounded so that He can begin to build more in you. So many Christians are flighty and airy. They say God has said certain things to them, but they never stick with something long enough to get grounded in their life. They are always learning, but they never come to the knowledge of the truth. They are constantly looking for a word, going from prophecy to prophecy. They have many prophecies, but they never get grounded enough to be able to conduct good warfare by using the prophecies. Those prophecies were given for a reason.

Paul told Timothy, "This charge I commit to you, son Timothy, according to the prophecies previously made concerning you, that by them you may wage the good warfare" (1 Tim. 1:18).

God wants you to get grounded so that things will manifest in your life. You want to bring things out of heaven into the earth in your life. For that to happen, you must be grounded.

But first, you must enter into the rest, because your greatest victories come out of rest, not out of self-effort. God wants to build a place of rest in you. Many people work themselves to the bone, trying to attain from their own strength what God has freely given by His grace.

To obtain heavenly things, and lay hold of them to bring them into the earthly realm, you must be grounded so that God can build kingdom ways in you. Jesus bridges the gap between where you lack, and where provision is in the Father. He makes the two into one so that you can learn how to operate in kingdom order. But, if you are running here and there, and fail to be grounded in Him, He cannot build those things in you.

Getting grounded means you have to die to self so you can access the treasures that are hidden in the dark. It's in the dark room that He develops you!

GOD DOES EVERYTHING IN THE DARK

Everything God does within you is done in the dark season of your life. God builds our destiny and calling through a series of seasons in our life. He takes us through a process of building things in us and removing things out of us.

To the degree that we are willing to stay in the dark with Him, and allow His image to be fashioned in us, is the degree to which we will walk in the fullness of our calling. Then, we will fulfill the purpose God has for us. God's purpose is to build His image in you. He wants you to stay the course of the process to become like Him-to be conformed and transformed to His image.

David allowed God to process him and fashion him into His image to bring forth His purposes in his life. We see in 1 Sam. 16:1-14 that God was doing a new thing. God was removing King Saul from his position and was going to appoint a new king, a king that He specifically chose, one that He could take through a process and build things in him.

God sets every member in the body in a place where He sees fit. It's not my choice as to what part I will be in the body. I get to choose to be the part that God wants me to be. To walk in your destiny, the best thing that you can do is surrender and yield to the place of God's choice for you. That is where your provision and anointing will be. The place and destiny God has for you is the most fulfilling and rewarding. He has created you to succeed on exceptionally high levels. That happens when you do His will that's in your heart-which is what He created you to do.

David's brothers did not get to choose to be king. David did not even get to choose to be king-God chose David to be king and David surrendered to the process, the plan, and the timing of God (1 Sam. 16:12-13).

As we pursue Jesus and engage in an intimate relationship with Him, His desire, and purpose for our life, becomes ours. But when we get into the world's way of thinking, the enemy will lie to you and tell you that the most prominent things are the most significant things. But, what God has called you to do is the most significant thing. It is His will, not ours.

Many never walk in the fullness of their calling, nor do they receive the fullness of all God has for them because they don't stay in the process. They don't surrender to the Father's will and His plan for their life. They don't pray, "Father your will be done." When you pray, "Father, your will be done and not mine," you become fully committed to His plan and purpose.

Even before you pray, you have to decide that your will is not what you're praying for. Jesus said when you pray say, "Our Father." When you pray this way, you go to the place in your life called the garden of Gethsemane. The place where Jesus says, "Not my will, but thine be done." When you are committed to do the will of God, and you pray only the will of God, every prayer will start being answered. I want to fulfill all He has called me to do. How about you?

God's will is His Word. You want to be sure that you are praying according to the Word. The Holy Spirit will never tell you to pray something that is contrary to the Word of God. I believe you know that, but it's worth repeating because it is so important.

Many never finish the process because they do not stay the course and allow their pastor to speak into their lives and bring correction and instruction. Stay in the process and let the Spirit of God build things in you so He can bring you to a place of Enlargement.

BUILDING BRINGS ENLARGEMENT

As we build things in the Spirit, we enlarge our spirit-we are preparing our spirit to receive a greater capacity of what God has for us. We build things in us by putting the Word in our mouth and declaring it by faith. However, the Word will not profit us unless you mix it with faith, so speak the Word with faith.

Our increase comes from the inside out. It is not so much what is happening on the outside, but what is happening on the inside, for increase to come. That is why it is imperative to build things in you with God's Word. God wants us to live by what He says in His Word, not by what we see. You must change your thinking, and what is on the inside will increase and prosper and manifest on the outside. Be God inside-minded; letting things work from the inside out.

There are times when we must come into that next season of our life that God has for us. We can even get into a place of distress where we cry out to God, "Do what You need to do to get me into that place you want me to be." Ps. 118:5 says, "From my distress I called upon the Lord. The Lord answered me and set me in a large place."

Many times, we cry out to the Lord in our distress. That distress can become a birthing place, or even a launching pad, to propel you into a new season with a new assignment. Faith not only has a voice, but it has a cry. We cry out to the Lord when we are tired of being in a place that never changes. The tight places in life can bring great distress and will make you cry out.

When you are in a narrow place, pressed in from all angles, and you are being squeezed, it will cause a cry of faith to come out of you. The tight, narrow places confine you and can be defined as limiting. It is in those places that God is building deep things in you.

It is in those times, in the weak moments, that the enemy comes to attack and bombard you with lies. Do not buy into the lies. Keep your shield of faith up; it will protect you from every fiery dart of the wicked one.

It is in those tight and narrow places that our roots go deep, and our faith grows exponentially. If things in your life are getting tighter on the outside, it's an indication that God wants to make you bigger on the inside. He wants to enlarge your capacity. He will awaken vision on the inside of you and begin to interest you. He will do that so you can see where He desires to enlarge you. Whenever God wants to enlarge you, He will give you a picture of it on the inside that will make faith come alive in your heart so that you can walk into it. God has to enlarge you on the inside before you enlarge on the outside. When you become enlarged inwardly, you will be positioned to receive the greater-the abundance He has for you.

God has got you in certain places because He desires for you to birth new things and bring those things forth. Only the

DESTINY ETCHED WITHIN

Spirit of God can tell you what those things are. That is why it is imperative to listen for His leading. You must hear His voice because enlargement comes with the ability to hear God and immediately obey and act on what He has said.

Stay in your place, do not get out of it. Stay in the process and let the Spirit of God build things in you so He can bring you to a place of enlargement.

It's in YOU!

188

CHAPTER FOURTEEN

DIVINE INTERRUPTIONS

There have been different seasons in my life that I knew I could not move forward in the things of God if I didn't take a risk and step out in faith. Several times I risked everything. The first time was when God called me to Rhema Bible College in Tulsa, Ok. In order to attend, I had to move from Oklahoma City. I still remember it like it was yesterday. I had given my resignation at the office a month in advance and before I knew it, my last day had arrived. I had mixed emotions - I was sad to leave my boss, co-workers, friends, and family, yet an excitement was exploding in me to start this new journey with the Lord. It was a big step of faith that required me to sell my house, my car and most of my furniture; but it was worth it all! Everything I gave up in order to move and attend Bible College, God blessed me exceedingly, and I never lacked for anything. It was amazing to see the supernatural hand of God bring provision to meet every need with plenty left over.

The second time I risked everything was when I was living in Dallas, Texas. I worked for a dental supply company and was doing very well. God had given me great favor with my regional manager and many representatives with the company. He was financially prospering me and opening many new doors of opportunity every which way I turned. It was a challenging, yet exciting time. I had extended family in that area that I only saw once a year while growing up. Little did I know what God had in store for all of us. He was about to open up the windows of Heaven to several of them and take them on a deeper journey with Him. It was glorious! Life was good!

One day, as I was driving to several appointments, I told the Lord I wanted everything He had for me. I wanted Him to do everything in me and through me that He desired to do. He told me, "It will require everything you have and complete obedience to My leading." It was that day the Lord said, "It's time to move back to Tulsa, OK for ministry. Quit your job, move to Tulsa by faith and I will show you the next step." Wow! God instructed me, once again to move and leave everything - career, family, friends, and Dallas shopping! I was to do so without knowing where I would work or how He would bring provision. In those moments, fear of the unknown will try its hardest to hold you back from taking that step, but I knew in my heart I had to take the risk to step into God's plan for my destiny and all He had put in my heart.

There have been many seasons of sacrifice to follow His leading for my life. But, I'm so glad I did because it has brought the greatest joy and rewards in my life-because He knows me better than I know myself.

STEP OUT IN FAITH

There was a great famine in Israel when judges ruled. A man from Bethlehem named Elimelech took his wife Naomi and his two sons and went to Moab to find food and decided to stay. Elimelech died, and Naomi continued to live with her two sons who married Moabite women named, Ruth and Orpah. They lived in Moab for ten years, then both sons died, leaving Naomi with her two-foreign daughter-in-laws.

A time came when God wanted to move Ruth and Naomi into a new thing in their lives, but it would require taking a big step of faith, and it was a risk. Ruth and Naomi had come to a place in their lives that they could not stay in the old season where they were. They knew there was no future for them there. God wanted to move them into greater things, but the only way He could do that was if they took a step of faith-to move forward into a new season of life. It was a risk, but they did it, and God brought forth an abundance of supply for their future.

What risk do you need to take today in order to experience the more God has for you? What opportunity is calling you to take bold steps on the journey toward the abundant life for which God created you? You have everything you need inside of you to take the next step.

TAKE ACTION

Destiny does not just happen in your life; destiny happens because you take action. There are things we must do to provoke the release of God's purpose in our lives. We may not know all of what God has placed within, but we must hunger for it, go after it to find it, and continue to move forward in it. Ruth and Naomi had to take some courageous steps to move forward. If Ruth had not chosen to go with Naomi, she would have missed the greatest blessing of her life. Stay faithful with whom God has told you to stay, and continue to honor them. Honor will take you places and open doors for you that you could never open for yourself. (More about honor in Chapter 15.)

Without question, we are called to move forward in life-if not literally then metaphorically-as we journey through life, and in our transformation in Christ. We cannot remain in that same place-meaning that place that never sees any change.

DIVINE INTERRUPTIONS

I have found that God is a God of divine interruptions. Divine interruptions from God can rapidly shift you from a season of barrenness into a season of birthing purpose. One visitation from God-just one touch from Him-and you immediately conceive what was not conceivable before.

MARY'S DIVINE INTERRUPTION

Mary had a divine interruption with Gabriel in Luke 1:26-27. God gives orders to Gabriel to visit Mary with a message. He shows up in Mary's life uninvited and interrupts her agenda. Mary was going about her business and having a normal day when all of the sudden a divine interruption happens with Gabriel. He interrupts Mary with a word, and he says, "Rejoice, highly favored one. The Lord is with you. Blessed are you among women" (Luke 1:28).

Are you willing to let God interrupt your space with His presence? Are you willing to let God interrupt you to birth something new and bring something fresh on the inside of you? Are you willing to have a divine interruption, and let God have His way in your life for His glory? God is looking for people who are willing to be interrupted.

Mary was just an ordinary girl. She was not a perfect girl, but she loved God. Mary needed a Savior just like you and me. What set Mary apart was that she was open. Mary opened her heart to whatever God desired to do in her life. When we open our heart, we leave margin in our life for a "divine interruption" from God. We are telling the Lord that we are open for Him to do something new, something fresh, and something totally divine of Him in our life.

I can only imagine what Mary was thinking. Gabriel has interrupted her, told her she is highly favored. In a sense, he was telling her that she was chosen to bring forth God's purpose.

Mary was about to conceive something that wasn't from herself, and it wasn't from man. What Mary was about to conceive was only from God. Mary didn't know that what she was carrying would impact and change the entire world. Mary questioned and asked how could this be? How is it going to come to pass in my life?

THE HOW QUESTION

Have there been times in your own life when you asked how? Times when you have been prophesied over, and you asked, "How will this ever happen?" Or maybe someone shared a vision with you and your immediate response was, how?

The How Question can get in the way of the Spirit of God with what He wants to do. Asking how can blind you from seeing the power of God in your life. Many times, we get so stuck at the how that it paralyzes us from moving forward into the new thing. How will camp out at a place called doubt and a place called fear?

Faith is always at the mountaintop and how is in the valley. How will always say, "I don't know how this miracle is going to happen."

"I don't know how my marriage is going to make it."

"I don't know how God is going to provide the finances and bring the supply that we need right now."

"I don't know how I am going to pay for school this semester."

"I don't know how I'm going to start this business or how I am going to take this business to the level."

Many camp out at how too long and miss the power of God and the miracle that God wants to do in their life. If you get out of your how-thinking, the Spirit of God will take you to the top of the mountain in His strength. You can't do it on your own, but the Spirit of God will come upon you, and what you were trying to do in the natural, God is going to do in the supernatural. The Spirit of God is going to show up in a divine way!

Mary could have started looking at all the reasons why she could not be used by God. Most people do this. We are too young, or we are too old. We do not have a college education. We lack resources and abilities. We look at ourselves and see lack. Then, we go from looking at who we are, to what we have done, and feel disqualified. Then, we lose heart.

After we give Him all the excuses, mistakes, and mishaps, God still wants to use us. No matter what you have done, God still wants to use you. He says, "I'm not finished with you." Because it's not about you, it's about the Spirit of God moving in you and through you for something that is meant to bless the world.

NOT JUST ABOUT YOU

Divine interruptions not only have to do with you, but they also have to do with those that are around you, starting with your family, friends, and coworkers. Many times, God has caused a divine interruption in my life to bring forth greater blessing in my family's life. He has used me to be an interrupting voice to speak life into a situation.

God wants to use you to be an interrupting voice of hope and faith in someone's fear. He wants to use you to be an interrupting voice of peace when there is strife. He has chosen YOU to do it!

GIDEON'S DIVINE INTERRUPTION

Gideon had a divine interruption with the angel. The Bible says in Judges 6:12, "And the Angel of the Lord appeared to him, and said to him, "The Lord is with you, you mighty man of valor!" They continued to carry on a dialogue, and the Lord told Gideon to save Israel from the Midianites that He would be with him.

God had an assignment for Gideon to carry out. Isn't it funny how sometimes it seems like we plead with God to help us, then when He shows up, we are totally amazed? Gideon did not believe in himself. He did not see in himself what God saw in him. After the angel called him a mighty warrior, Gideon said, "Who me?"

It seems God shows up in our lives, not only to bless us and guide us, but He shows up in our lives to help us discover what He has placed inside us that we do not even know is there. Let the Spirit of God interrupt you and show you what He has placed inside of you. It is a new season for you.

ESTHER'S DIVINE INTERRUPTION

Esther was a young Jewish orphan girl living in a foreign land, and the king chose her to be his queen. After Esther became queen, an evil man named Hamon, plotted to kill all the Jews. He deceived the king into writing a decree stating that all the Jewish people would be exterminated. The decree was sent out across the land. When Esther's uncle, Mordecai, heard about it, he cried out to His God to save their people.

Esther had a divine interruption in her life. God knew what He put in her, and He wanted to use her as an interrupting voice to bring deliverance to a nation. In Esther 4:8, Mordecai gave Esther a charge to save her people. I'm sure Esther didn't think she had it in her to carry out such a courageous assignment. I'm sure she asked, "How" can I do this?" Yet, a season had come upon Esther, and for such a time as this, she was charged to take an assignment of God. God was calling her to come up higher and fully answer the call of that assignment.

Esther did not choose that assignment, nor the battle she was about to walk into. However, God had anointed her for the task, and Esther rose up in strength and courage for the battle in which she found herself. She accepted the assignment; she moved into a new place; into a new season that God destined for her and her people. In order for her to come into that place, she had to hear what the Spirit of the God was saying to her in that crisis hour.

JOSEPH'S DIVINE INTERRUPTION

Joseph was marked by destiny-he was marked by God. Joseph didn't know what all was inside him, but God did. God placed favor on Joseph's life that elevated him to a position of power that he never experienced. Joseph encountered many disheartening situations, but he remained faithful, even through all the adverse circumstances. Joseph remained strong and never allowed himself to become a victim. He never felt sorry for himself.

It is important that in your circumstances, you see yourself as the victor, not the victim. You must rise above and get the Father's perspective on the matter. If you buy into the lie that you are a victim, the enemy will defeat you every time.

Joseph never gave up hope on God's redemptive power in his life. He had an intimate relationship with God, and because he did, He knew his God well. Joseph daily communed with Him and made an exchange with Him; therefore, he knew God had not abandoned him. Joseph made the most of every situation and never gave up.

If you feel forgotten, know this-God has not forgotten you. He has been preparing you. I'm sure there were many times Joseph could have felt forgotten and forsaken. Pharaoh's butler forgot about him, and Joseph remained in prison for a few more years (Gen. 40:23). Since God knows all things, all the time, I believe God allowed the butler to forget about Joseph until His divine timing was right for Joseph to step into the fulfillment of his destiny.

The favor on Joseph's life had taken him from the pit that his brothers threw him into, to a place where he became a slave. Unbeknownst to Joseph, later he would even find himself in prison. The Bible says in Prov. 18:16, "A man's gift makes room for him and brings him before great men." This is exactly what Joseph experienced in his life. His gift of interpreting dreams led him from the pit of the prison to the high places in the palace. Because Joseph was fully committed to God's faithfulness, the favor that was on his life eventually propelled him into the fullness of his identity and his divine destiny.

Joseph trusted in God, which caused a divine appointment with destiny to arrive. Because Joseph walked in a place of trust with God, opportunity knocked on his door, and Joseph was ready to respond because he had allowed God to do a deep work in him. That deep work prepared Joseph for anything he would come up against. I believe he knew in his heart God would cause an opportunity to present itself to him; therefore, he prepared himself, and he purposed to be faithful through everything.

YOUR NEXT STEP

What about you? Are you ready to take the next step in fulfilling your destiny? If an opportunity knocked at your door today, would you be prepared, willing, and ready to respond and step through that door? What has God been talking to you about lately? What has He been charging you with? What has been tugging on your heart?

God wants to propel you into the fullness of your true identity and your divine destiny. Begin to prepare yourself so that you are ready for that divine interruption He's bringing your way. It is an opportunity that God is setting up just for you. He knows what is inside you, while you do not. You have it in you; you are empowered to do the impossible and accomplish the task He puts before you.

The enemy will do whatever it takes to distract you - to distract your hearing and to distract you from envisioning what your spirit is perceiving. Guard what you hear; guard what you allow in your spirit. The Bible says to incline your ear unto His sayings (Prov. 4:20-22).

Allow yourself quality time with Him so the Spirit of God can show you things in your spirit (John 16:13). He will cause thoughts and ideas to come up in your spirit that you have never seen before. You will know it is Him because you would have never thought of it on your own.

God is calling forth His Ruths, Esthers, Marys, and Josephs to arise and take their assignments. He is calling you to take your place. Will you accept the charge? Get ready for some divine interruptions! Tell the Lord you are willing to be a divine interruption for Him!

It's in YOU!

CHAPTER FIFTEEN

STAY IN A PLACE OF HONOR

I truly believe honor is most essential in life to reach the heights of all God has for you in life. Without honor, you will not succeed and achieve your dreams.

One of my most favorite things to do is to honor people and overwhelm them with the appreciation of love. It truly brings me great joy to not only speak words of honor over my elders but also over my peers. The Lord has shown me personally how we honor one another affects the entire atmosphere around us. Paul says in Romans 12:10, "Be devoted to one another in love. Honor one another above yourselves." I am convinced we are to live in an atmosphere of honor!

Honor and respect are characteristics of heaven, and we are to bring heaven to earth. When an atmosphere of honor is created, life and favor flourishes. When we walk in a place of honor, we invite new life and fresh favor into our lives. As we celebrate and honor one another, an atmosphere is created allowing God to do the miraculous in our lives. In that atmosphere, God can restore and align hearts in seconds what might take years in the natural.

The Lord interested me in an opportunity to honor someone above and beyond any way I had honored a person before. He spoke to my heart His desire of me and impressed on me that through my obedience to His word, He would cause many amazing things to happen. I went shopping with my pastor for some supplies concerning the church. While shopping together, the Lord spoke to my heart that He wanted me to wash her feet. When I heard that from Him, it caught me off guard only because that was the first time I had heard Him say anything like that. It stopped me in my tracks, and I said, "What Lord?" He said it again and expounded, "I want you to wash her feet, and through your humility and honor toward her, I will do some miraculous things." Then He said, "Familiarity breeds contempt-don't allow yourself to get too familiar, but humble yourself and honor her, then watch what I will do."

After we finished shopping, I told Pastor Brenda what the Lord put on my heart to do. By the look on her face, I could tell she was just as surprised as I was. She looked at me with a funny look and then said, "Okay." At that point, I think we both knew God had something special and amazing in mind. We went inside her house, and I gathered the things I needed. As I started washing her feet and honoring her, all of the sudden the presence of God flooded the room! In seconds, the weighty presence of His glory was in the room and all over us!

I began to speak words of blessing and honor over her, and as I did, His presence and power intensified and the weight of His glory literally froze us in one spot. I could not pick up my hands and move them anymore; nor could I move my head. This seemed to last for quite some time as God was ministering to our hearts. I was astonished by everything God did in that moment. Areas in my heart that needed touched, were healed within seconds. Any areas that needed a slight adjustment, got adjusted. Father's love encapsulated us and saturated us in a way that I cannot describe in words. It was glorious! It all happened because I walked in obedience to the voice of God to honor her in a greater way than I ever had before. After a few minutes of speaking words over her, no words were needed as my honor spoke without saying a word.

FAMILIARITY BREEDS CONTEMPT

Honor is a key component and essential in life. It speaks without ever saying a word. To honor someone means to value, to highly esteem, to see as precious. Honor also means to highly respect and revere. In the Gospel of Mark, we see that Jesus was rejected in his hometown of Nazareth.

But Jesus said to them, "A prophet is not without honor except in his own country, among his own relatives, and

in his own house." Now He could do no mighty work there,
except that He laid His hands on a few sick people and
healed them. And He marveled because of their unbelief.
Then He went about the villages in a circuit, teaching.

MARK. 6:4-6 (NKJV)

I'm sure you have heard the old saying, familiarity breeds contempt. It is difficult for a prophet to do miracles or healings in his home town. These people were too familiar with Jesus the carpenter, the son of Joseph and Mary. They did not see Him as a precious gift sent from God. They did not place value on the gift that was in Him. They saw him as a common ordinary man. They saw him in his natural abilities. For those who did not value the gift he was, they missed the supernatural in their life. Because they withheld honor, God's will and His supply were restricted.

APPRECIATE THE GIFTS

I was reflecting on the divine connections God had given me, and those who are dear to my heart. The Spirit of God began to speak to me encouraging me not to miss the fullness of the gifts they are in my life. But, for me to highly esteem and place great value and honor on the gift that is resident within them.

I once heard a man telling how God had used his father-in-the-faith in extraordinary ways, even though he was a humble and ordinary man. Because this person saw his mentor only as ordinary, and did not highly esteem and honor the gift that he was, he missed this minister's greatness. Later, he regretted this oversight.

This pierced my heart and brought conviction! It took me to another place of humility. The Spirit of God opened my eyes to see on a grander scale to place even higher honor, more than I had before, on the gift in pastors, ministers, and other people He has placed in my life. To not look upon them as ordinary, like the people of Nazareth saw Jesus. God said to me, "You will receive revelation and insight to the degree that you honor the gift-the person."

That day, I purposed in my heart I would honor them-to the highest level that I knew how-and not miss their greatness. I determined that from that point forward, I would give honor where honor was due. Also, I would draw on the gifts that they are to me, and receive all God has for me through them.

Never miss an opportunity to honor. Choose to carry a spirit of honor about yourself and make it your standard with all people. For when you honor them, you are honoring God Himself. In the words of 1 Samuel 2:30, the Lord declares, "...I will honor those who honor me..."

Be mindful of honoring your pastors, parents, spiritual parents, family members, co-workers, and friends. Do not miss the greatness God has placed inside of them. Purpose in your heart to honor that gift and receive all God has for you because you will receive revelation and insight to the degree that you honor.

Honor people for the position they hold and the gift they carry to the body of Christ. The Bible says in Eph. 4:8 that "God gave gifts unto men." In verses 11 and 12, it says, "And He Himself gave some apostles, some prophets, some evangelists, and some pastors and teachers, for the equipping of the saints for the work of ministry, for the edifying of the body of Christ." God's design is that the person encompasses the gift. They are the gift that God appoints to carry important gifts and functions.

GIFTS OF GOD CONNECTED TO HONOR

Many people get stuck in life and come to a standstill on their journey because they have become familiar with what they used to honor. The gifts of God are connected with honor. When we become familiar with something and don't honor it to the degree that it should be honored, revelation will be hindered from flowing to us through that gift. Wisdom, insight, instruction, and direction from the Spirit of God are hindered from flowing to you, and you need those gifts to propel you further into God's plan for your life. When you cease to honor a gift (special person) that is a voice in your life, that voice will lose its power to speak into your life.

Many people are not even aware of the importance of honoring and praying for their pastors, and how it is directly related to the revelation and guidance from the Spirit of God concerning their life. If we do not honor the office and gift that is placed before us, we miss out. Many don't realize that God has prepared and supplied that gift from which they are to receive. They do not realize they are really receiving from God, not the man or women who deliver the message. When you honor the gift as God speaking to you, you position yourself to receive revelation from God. To the degree you honor and believe, you will receive. If the way in which you give honor is small and minuscule, that is the measure you will receive in return. But, if you give honor to a great degree, you open yourself, and your heart, to receive an abundant supply from God.

Notice what the Apostle Paul has to say about honor:

> *But we request of you, brethren, that you appreciate those who diligently labor among you, and have charge over you in the Lord and give you instruction, and that you esteem them very highly in love because of their work. Live in peace with one another.* 1 THESS. 5:12, 13 (NKJV)

The word esteem means to deem highly or to consider highly. In other words, you could say, "I highly esteem you." Notice it says to esteem them very highly. This means super abundantly, or excessively. God's desire is revealed in these scriptures towards those who are in ministry.

I believe that it is vital to value the ministry gifts and to honor them the way God sees them. We are not looking to a man or woman of God from a natural standpoint; we are looking at the gifts and callings God has placed within them.

When you honor and respect the gifts, then you will be able to operate in the highest level of anointing and calling that God has given you.

ELISHA HONORED ELIJAH

The prophet Elisha honored the prophet Elijah by staying very close to him. In fact, toward the end of Elijah's life, when he announced that he was about to depart from the world, Elisha cried out and said, "I pray thee, let a double portion of thy spirit be upon me" (2 Kings 2:9). Elisha was saying, let the anointing that is on you come upon me in a double portion. Elijah said, "Yet if you see me when I am taken from you, it will be yours-otherwise, it will not" (2 Kings 2:10).

Elijah was telling Elisha that he needed to get close to him and stay focused on him so that the anointing that was on Elijah could come upon Elisha. Elijah let Elisha know that if he got distracted and lost focus by taking his eyes off of him, the anointing would not come upon him. Elisha took Elijah as his word and stayed focused with his eyes fixed on Elijah. When Elijah was taken away, Elisha saw him and received a double portion of Elijah's anointing.

David walked in a place of honor toward King Saul when he spared his life (1 Sam. 24). Joseph walked in honor when he refused to lie with Potiphar's wife (Gen. 39:7-10). Job walked in honor when he refused to curse God and die (Job 2:9-10). Joseph walked in honor when he chose to stay with Mary when she was pregnant with Jesus (Matt. 1:19-20).

ORDER OF RELATIONSHIPS

There is a strong order of relationships in the Bible. We are to respect our elders so that the stability and the wisdom that has been upon them can come upon our life. It is true in the natural and the supernatural. I admonish you to guard yourself against the law of familiarity and be careful that you do not develop a contempt for your pastor or those that God has placed in your life that is your spiritual leaders. Be careful to not take them or their sermons for granted and lose the opportunity to receive more of the anointing that is on them.

You should have purpose in your life to see and honor the gift in the minister, then draw on that. When you do, God is able to release more revelation to you. When we draw on the gift and expect to get something from God, the limitations are immeasurable. When you are drawing on the gift, you are drawing on the gift of God within that person, which allows God to move and speak through that person to you.

Paul says, in 1 Tim. 5:17, "The elders who perform their leadership duties well are to be considered worthy of double honor (financial support), especially those who work hard at preaching and teaching [the word of God concerning eternal salvation through Christ]." (AMP)

He goes on to say in 1 Tim. 6:1 that we are to give honor to those who teach us the Word: "Let all who are under the yoke as bond servants esteem their own [personal] masters worthy of honor and fullest respect, so that the name of God and the teaching [about Him] may not be brought into disrepute and blasphemed."

We are to give ministers of the gospel twice as much honor

as we would any other leader or person. Double honor. Walk in a place of utmost respect for them, listening intently for wisdom and insight. Know that the Spirit of God will speak to you through them to give you guidance in a matter you may be facing now, or one you may face in the future.

HONOR AND RECEIVING

Honor is an essential key to receiving from God. 1 Sam. 2:30 says, "...for those who honor Me I will honor, and those who despise Me shall be lightly esteemed." We must first honor God, and then He says He will honor us. We find in the Bible that everyone who honored Jesus received a supernatural supply from Him. They received to the degree that they honored Him.

Jesus says in John 13:20, "He who receives me receives him who sent me." Jesus is saying that the person who honors Jesus, honors the Father who sent Him. He is also saying that when you receive someone-when, you open your heart to them and welcome them-you are honoring Him.

This is God's design of how honor operates and flows.

He who receives you receives Me, and he who receives Me receives Him who sent Me. He who receives a prophet in the name of a prophet shall receive a prophet's reward. And he who receives a righteous man in the name of a righteous man shall receive a righteous man's reward. And whoever gives one of these little ones only a cup of cold water in the name of a disciple, assuredly, I say to you, he shall by no means lose his reward. MATT. 10:40-42 (NKJV)

God is a God of order, and He appoints authority. In God's kingdom, there is rank, order, and delegated authority. There is an order in which God operates; we are obligated to line up with that order. When you submit to the authority in your life, you align yourself with His order of operation. As a child of God, your spirit will recognize and esteem authority. A person who knows God will be one who recognizes the Father's authority.

HONOR STRANGERS

Another way to give honor is to bless someone who is a total stranger. I have done this for years, especially in the Christmas season. One Christmas, the Lord prompted me to bless people I didn't know in different stores. While they were in line and the checker was checking them out, the Lord had me ask them if it was okay if I paid for their things. I told them that this was a gift from God and that He loved them.

At the end of that same week, I received a check in the mail from my mortgage lender. The letter stated that I had been over-charged four years ago when I purchased my home. I cannot recall anything they might have overcharged me with, but I was rejoicing. That check for $755 paid for a set of new tires that I needed. Glory to God!

He showed me that even when I honor people who are strangers to me, He blesses that and multiplies it exponentially back to me. He is a good and an extravagant God!

DOORS OF OPPORTUNITY

Honor is the seed that will open great doors of opportunities-doors you never imagined would open. When you recognize God's authority and walk in honor, it positions your heart to be fully open to the possibilities of God flowing in your life. Walking in a place of honor opens doors of opportunities for promotion. It opens the door for God to place you in a position of leadership and authority for His purposes.

Walking in a place of honor will also shut the door to the enemy in your life. It stops any opportunity for him to channel thoughts of strife, envy, discord, and jealousy towards another person. As I often say, "Give no place to the devil to operate in your life." Eph. 4:27 says, "nor give place to the devil." That means you can give place to things in your life. Walking in a place of honor becomes a protection over you.

In the Kingdom of God, we are called to serve one another. It is all about serving in the Kingdom. When we honor people, we serve them. It is a two-way flow, and each will be more effective in what they are designed to do, as well as being pleasing to God. It pleases Him when we honor and serve one another. When we walk in that place of honor, blessings will truly chase you down.

Jesus not only demonstrated honor to leaders and those in authority, but he gave honor to those who had no honor and were dishonored in their life. He reached out to them and demonstrated His love with great compassion.

1 Pet. 2:17 tells us to: "Honor all men. Love the brotherhood. Fear God. Honor the king."

The Amplified version says: "Show respect for all people [treat them honorably], love the brotherhood [of believers], fear God, honor the king."

The Message version says: "Treat everyone you meet with dignity. Love your spiritual family. Revere God. Respect the government."

Loving people will keep you in a place of honor in your life. Love always takes the high road. Love and honor will always call us to walk in His highest and best for our lives.

We should not become complacent in honoring men and women in the faith. Appreciate and draw upon their wisdom when they are willing to open up and share their own experiences. For it will help you see things that could make a huge difference in your life and could alter the course of your destiny.

This is imperative for where the Lord desires to take you in this season.

Humility and honor go hand-in-hand. To walk in a place of honor, you must walk in a place of humility. There is an element of humility that sets your self aside and looks to honor others.

It's in YOU!

CHAPTER SIXTEEN

KNOW WHAT YOU CARRY

I t was an ordinary day, but God had something extraordinary in mind. It was a beautiful morning as I sat in the presence of the Lord with my coffee and my Bible. I was seeking the Lord and praying about a few things when He began to put a person on my heart. He ministered to me about this person and impressed upon me that I was to visit her at her house that afternoon. This person was going through an intense battle physically that was taking a toll on them mentally and emotionally, causing her to sink into a severe depression. Not only did she need encouragement, but she needed a powerful touch from God, and she needed it NOW! The Lord gave me specific instructions to completely shift the atmosphere in her home upon my arrival and to release Him into the situation. Being a carrier of the glory of God, as soon as I stepped into her house, I began to release the presence and the peace of God with my words. I took my authority in the name of Jesus and broke off that spirit of depression that was tracking her, keeping her entangled and bound. I began to pray for her, lay my hands on her, and release the power of God into her body to cause healing and a cure. The power of God was all over her! Her body began to shake under the power as God was touching her and doing a mighty work. This was her day of deliverance, and God chose to use me as the carrier to release Him into that situation. What a glorious day it was, for she was delivered and set free, encouraged and healed as God showed up on the scene!

WHAT RESIDES WITHIN YOU

Are you aware of what you carry inside of you? Do you know what God has deposited inside you that will bring life to hurting people? We have the power to change and create an atmosphere of Heaven. We carry that on the inside of us.

You are a carrier of the presence and the glory of God. You are a carrier of The Blessing. It is as if the Ark of the Covenant resides inside you. Everywhere you go, you carry Him. You carry His life, His presence, His peace, His hope, and His love. You carry His power and He wants to use you to be a demonstration of Himself-to release His power and presence wherever you go.

You carry His presence; therefore, you can alter the environment to bring a shift and a change, simply by stepping into the

216

room. What you become aware of, you are positioned to release.

Jesus said the Kingdom of God is within you, and it can be released in many different ways (Luke 17:21). It is released through touch, prophetic acts, and words. In John 6:63, Jesus says, "...the words that I speak unto you, they are spirit, and they are life." Jesus is the Word of God made flesh. Every time He spoke, the Word of God became spirit-it became life. Why is that important?

In Rom. 14:17, Paul tells us that "the Kingdom of God is not meat or drink, but righteousness, peace, and joy in the Holy Ghost." The Kingdom of God is in the Holy Spirit, and when words become spirit, God's dominion is released over people. That means, when we tap into the heart of the Father, and we say what He is saying, we impart His Spirit, His life, His presence and His power through our words. When your words are Spirit, they bring Life!

YOU ARE THE CARRIER OF DESTINY

Not only are you a carrier of the presence of God and all His attributes, but God has made you to carry destiny. He has made you to carry a dream. He has made you to carry purpose. However, your destiny will not just be handed to you. Most of what you need in life will be brought to you, but you have to go after what you want in life. For you to come into your destiny, there is a fight that must be won and it is a fight of persistence and diligence. It is knowing how to strengthen and encourage yourself in the middle of a battle of confusion. These are essential in building us to help us holdfast until the answer and clarity comes.

The Bible is full of men and women who carried destiny. They had to go after it before they could come into it. First, they had to know what they carried. Then, they had to step into it and release it.

BIBLE EXAMPLES

Joshua carried a spirit of faith to lead the people of Israel into the Promised Land. Abraham carried a spirit of faith, for He was the father of faith. Mary carried the Promise, Jesus the King who would be the Savior of the world. Elizabeth carried the one who would prepare a nation to meet Jesus-John the Baptist. John the Baptist carried the message that prepared a nation to meet Jesus.

Elijah carried a message that urged the people of Israel to turn from sin and to return to the true God. God appointed him to go before kings and bring the message of warning and repentance. Elisha, his successor, carried on the message and did almost everything Elijah did, only twice as much.

Paul carried revelation of the church and brought forth much of our understanding of Christianity. He bridged the gap between Jews and Gentiles by demonstrating that the way of Jesus was open to anyone, regardless of ancestry.

Think about what it might be like today if Paul brought his supply and spoke forth the revelation that God put within him concerning the church. What he was carrying was life-changing to those to heard him back then, and it continues to us today. Likewise, the supply you and I carry is important and life-changing and has the potential to affect thousands, even millions, all around the world.

Isaiah carried prophecies for his day, then moved forward to a far greater fulfillment of prophecies about Jesus Christ, addressing both Jesus' first and second comings.

Jeremiah carried a message to the nations urging a change of heart and turning to the one true God. God gave Jeremiah the overview of his prophetic ministry: "Behold, I have put My words in your mouth. See, I have this day set you over the nations and the kingdoms, to root out and to pull down, to destroy and to throw down, to build and to plant" (Jer. 1:9, 10). Just like Jeremiah, I believe God has put His words in our mouths to bring deliverance, healing, and restoration to a hurting world.

Nehemiah carried a vision with a strong conviction and determination to rebuild the walls of Jerusalem. He was positioned for the purpose at a specific time. God placed Nehemiah in a position to serve the king, who at that time was the most powerful ruler in the known world. God positioned Nehemiah there to accomplish God's will and purpose. Nehemiah was carrying a vision inside him to rebuild the walls of Jerusalem. Eventually, the king consented to his request, appointed him governor of Judea, and sent him to his beloved city of Jerusalem. Nehemiah worked tirelessly to rebuild the walls despite continual opposition.

Miraculously, the wall was completed in fifty-two days. He

would not allow himself to be deterred from his vision, even when his enemies scoffed at him and threatened to take his life. Nehemiah set the high standard that God required, even if it meant personal loss, discomfort, or pain. He knew he was positioned to accomplish God's will and purpose.

Likewise, God has positioned you right where you need to be to bring forth something that is inside of you. You are carrying His purpose, and it is time for it to be birthed. It is time for you to step into that dream to start that business, or ministry, or career that you have longed for. It's time for you to deliver that word that you have been carrying. Do not hold back! I challenge you to take bold steps and let it come forth. Know what you carry and let it out!

POWER OF ASSOCIATION

In light of the fact that within you, you carry your destiny; it is very important who you associate with. Who surrounds you within your inner circle? With whom do you share your dreams and passions?

When you encounter someone, who is doing what is on the inside of you, your spirit almost explodes with excitement, because that connection speaks to you. In a sense, they are speaking your language! They are carriers and releasers of what is in you; therefore, you easily track with them. The deep wells in that person will speak to the deep wells in you. God uses them as a catalyst to open up your thinking and enlarge your dreams so

He can show you your potential. He uses that moment to draw out the deep places in you.

They say that you become like the five people with whom you associate the most. Think about your associations. Who are you around? Are you around people who build you up and speak life into you? Are you around people who love you unconditionally and think the best of you? Those who want the best for you?

Or are your friends and associates the type of people who drain you, and are always negative? The type of people who kill your dreams.

Your associations are powerful. It is important that you build the right associations around you. You need to surround yourself with people who will challenge you; separate yourself from people who are reinforcing negative belief systems. Know when to let go. Do not force what does not fit in your life anymore. Do not hold on to something because of fear o change. Change may not always be fun because it can feel like a loss. But, that fear can be faced and conquered.

There are people in your life who are like rocket boosters-they go up in that first atmosphere with you, and then they fall off your life. The space shuttle that tries to keep on going to the next stratosphere with the rocket boosters still attached is headed for a crash. Sometimes, we keep people in our lives past their expiration date. That does not necessarily mean that is a bad thing. It is just not God's best for you at this time.

Consider who is in your life. Where do you spend your time? What relationships do you nurture? What caliber of people do you have around you? A true friend can see you at your worst and still believe the best in you. They help bring the best out, and they help celebrate that.

It's important that you keep your inner circle small. The devil accomplishes more in your life through infiltration than he ever will through confrontation. His purpose is to come into your life and pollute or dilute. If he can pollute your commitment, your purity and dilute your effectiveness, he destroys your influence.

SHIFTS OF GOD

It is very important you guard your inner circle of relationships because God is about to shift you. Our times are changing, and if you do not shift with the times and seasons, you will get run over. Can you imagine driving a standard car and only driving in first gear the entire time? You can tell by the sound of the engine when it's time to shift. When you shift, you increase in speed. That means on this next level, the things that took you a long time to get started and off the ground in the first dimension, are getting ready to have accelerated results as you step into this next season.

As you shift, God will cause things to begin to move faster. It always takes longer with the groundwork and foundational time. This is a prophetic time for a divine shifting in your life! Your season is about to shift! Seasons don't shift just because of the passage of time. There are people that have gotten old, and nothing has shifted for them. They are still in the same place.

Your seasons shift because either a person enters or exits your life. When a single woman marries a single man, their season shifts. It was not because of the passage of time; it was because of a person coming into their life. It was about who came into her life. They moved from being single into marriage and their season changed overnight. You can be a married couple and the moment that you have a baby, your season shifts because a baby was born. When a woman has lived her life with her husband, and all of the sudden her husband dies, her season changes. Your season is determined by who enters and exits your life.

When Elijah met Elisha, Elijah threw his cloak over Elisha and said follow me. His season shifted. It had nothing to do with the calendar. It was because of who stepped into Elisha's life. Our season changes when Jesus steps in! It was because of WHO that stepped in that transformed something on the inside!

Whenever God allows you to meet your WHO, your life gets ready to go to a brand new level. God will bring people on a different level into your life. The realm of the influence of the relationship will change in your life. That is why David had to meet Jonathan. David was a country boy. He knew nothing about the etiquette of operating in the king's palace. Jonathan was a king's kid. He was raised in the palace, and he understood the etiquette of the kingdom. But David didn't know anything, and it was when Jonathan came into David's life that his life shifted because of who came into his life.

It was when Moses came to Pharaoh that a season changed.

It was when David was introduced to Goliath. It wasn't Goliath that made David. Goliath exposed that champion that was in David. Sometimes, God will even use your enemy when it is time to promote you into your next season with God.

Don't ever be confused about it when God begins to shift you, and there is something that happens. It's the divine power of God using a relationship to step into your life to cause a destiny movement! A defining moment! A moment where your life will not be like business, as usual, any longer because of WHO came into your life. The WHO is always more important than the WHAT!

POWERFUL EXAMPLE OF ASSOCIATION

One of my favorite examples in the Bible is the story of Mary and Elizabeth. Mary gets pregnant by the overshadowing of the Holy Spirit. This was a time in which, culturally, a woman getting pregnant outside of marriage meant she was to be stoned to death. That was the law. Mary probably couldn't even go to her parents. However, Mary had a cousin named Elizabeth, and the Holy Spirit told her to go to Elizabeth's house.

Mary arrives at Elizabeth's house, and when she sees Elizabeth, it was so powerful that her baby leaps on the inside of her; and the same happens for Elizabeth's baby on the inside of her. When that happened, the scripture says Elizabeth was filled with the Holy Spirit (Luke 1:41). This is a reminder that when God is doing something greater in your life, He sends the right people for you to hook up and associate with.

Mary stayed with Elizabeth for most of her pregnancy. I have realized when you are with the right people, they are not threatened by you, and they do not try to compete with you. I believe Elizabeth celebrated Mary and the seed of purpose that was in her, which was going to bring forth life to the whole world. Elizabeth, too, had a promise within her that would bring forth its purpose. Elizabeth recognized she carried something different, but it was still needed for the plan and the purpose of God. The purpose she carried would make way for the coming of the Lord. Mary was carrying Jesus the Messiah, the Son of God who would eventually save the world.

As it was with Mary, so shall the power of the Most High overshadow you and cause you to give birth to the dreams and destiny you are carrying. It will be in His perfect timing for His glory.

What you are carrying has greatness written all over it. The determination of whether that greatness will be celebrated, honored or even understood, depends on who you are associating with.

Make a quality decision about the people with whom you choose to fellowship; those with whom you will surround yourself.

Allow some of your time to be spent with people who are more advanced, more knowledgeable, and more anointed than you. By doing so, you will be more anointed, advanced, and knowledgeable than if you spend all your time with people who are on your same level. They have a lot to do with the destiny you live out and where you are in life. Choose people who see the potential of God in you. Associate yourself with those who are carriers of the dream inside of you. Draw on that gift that is within them and allow God to open up your supply and go for it!

It's in YOU!

CONCLUSION

Recently, I was watching television and came across a show where they were restoring old cars. I was not particularly interested in watching it, but the Spirit of God quickened me to keep watching it. It is amazing to see how someone can take an old junky car that is rusted and corroded, and not only restore it back to its original value, but increase its value by adding new items and techniques into the restoration of the vehicle.

To me, it just looked like a piece of junk, but to the trained eye, the one who is the expert (because they know exactly what the original car looked like), they see the value, worth, and beauty.

I am reminded of a famous Caravaggio painting that was lost for about 200 years but was rediscovered hanging in the Dublin Jesuits' dining room. The painting, The Taking of Christ, was a masterpiece by the famous and influential Italian Baroque master, Michelangelo Merisi da Caravaggio.

For many years, it had been wrongly identified as a painted replica by another artist, and as a result, it had been devalued. Its authenticity was questioned, but as layers of dirt and discolored varnish was removed, the quality and value of the painting were revealed. This painting that was once thought to be a replica with minimal value became an extremely valuable priceless treasure.

There are several TV shows where valuable treasures are discovered in what people thought looked like worthless junk. These shows are great because they remind us that things that may appear to look ordinary or of no value, are priceless, rare and valuable.

Similarly, we often need to be reminded of our value and the priceless treasure God placed inside of us. As we go through seasons in our lives, we encounter different challenges that sometimes cause us to forget who we are.

As you have read this book, I hope you have been stirred in your spirit to not give up on your dream and all that God has for you. I hope you see your true identity and authenticity. You are His masterpiece, an original and priceless valuable work of art. His eye is on you, and His plan is to restore you back to your original and priceless value.

The Bible says that God is perfecting those things, which concern you. He is constantly doing a work in us. Perfecting us. God has a plan of significance, purpose, and abundance for your life. His word says, "Blessed are they that put their trust in Him"

(Ps. 2:12). As you put your trust in Him and follow the leading of the Spirit, He will cause you to prosper and flourish.

His Word says He will make known to us the mystery of His will according to His good pleasure (Eph. 1:9). The vital key is, knowing Him. You will never know who you are, or what you are called to do until you first know Him.

If you don't know God's plan and purpose for your life, I challenge you to worship Him. As you do, He will tell you who you are and what He has put inside of you. He will reveal the gifts He has deposited in you and what He has called you to do.

God is calling you into a new season. Enlarge yourself and move into the new. You are well able to take the land He places before you. Walk with confidence knowing everything you need He has already placed within you.

It's in YOU!

ABOUT THE AUTHOR

Shonna ministers the gospel in a passionate and powerful way. She encourages individuals to know the Spirit of Truth and His power that is available to believers today. She also encourages individuals to know who they are in Christ and instructs them how to operate in faith from that revelation. Shonna's lifestyle and ministry demonstrate how to pursue the presence of God and encourage many to fulfill their personal calling. Her practical teaching inspires God's people to follow their heart and dreams, knowing that God has put in them all that they need to do the impossible for the assignment at hand.

At a young age, Shonna sensed a divine purpose and calling on her life. She knew God had destined her for greatness, to have an impact on lives by being a voice for Him, but didn't yet have a full understanding of what that meant. After embracing this sense of divine purpose, she was determined to whole-heartedly pursue the calling that would ultimately steer the course of the rest of her life.

After having an encounter with God, her path eventually led her to Rhema Bible College where she graduated in 2001. Later, in 2004, she attended and graduated from the Schambach School of Ministries. She has traveled to the nations ministering in churches, women's meetings, Bible schools, and crusades.

Shonna also has experience in the corporate world, working as a sales representative for a dental supply company. Additionally, she has served as a spokesperson for several non-profit organizations, emceeing various events.

In the local church, she has served as a worship leader, in women's ministry, cooperate prayer leader and children's ministry, as well as ministering on a local cable TV network. She currently attends The Calling Church in Norman, Ok where she ministers.

Shonna has a passion to encourage people to pursue the presence of God and the purpose and calling on their life. Her desire is for people to live intentional lives empowered by the knowledge of who they are in Christ, and to know the ways and the person of the Holy Spirit.

Shonna has worked as a dental hygienist for 23 years. She received her Bachelor of Science degree at the University of Oklahoma. She currently practices as a hygienist part-time and resides in Norman, Oklahoma.